HUNGRY FOR HOPE?

Nick Baines

SAINT ANDREW PRESS
Edinburgh

First published in 1991 by
Daybreak
Darton, Longman & Todd Ltd
89 Lillie Road, London SW6 1UD

This new and updated edition first published in 2007 by
SAINT ANDREW PRESS
121 George Street, Edinburgh EH2 4YN

Copyright © Nick Baines, 2007

ISBN 978-0-7152-0844-1

British Library Cataloguing in Publication Data
A catalogue record for this book is available from the British Library.

It is the Publisher's policy to only use papers that are natural and recyclable
and that have been manufactured from timber grown in renewable, properly
managed forests. All of the manufacturing processes of the papers are expected
to conform to the environmental regulations of the country of origin.

Typeset in Baskerville by Waverley Typesetters, Fakenham
Printed and bound by Bell & Bain Ltd, Glasgow

CONTENTS

ACKNOWLEDGEMENTS

The Scriptural quotations are taken from The Holy Bible, New International Version, copyright © 1973, 1978, 1984 International Bible Society, published by Hodder & Stoughton Ltd. The quotations from *Wild Goose Songs* and *The Iona Communiy Worship Book* are copyright Wild Goose Publications, The Iona Community, Scotland.

FOREWORD

It was a damp, dark and drizzly Friday evening. A group of teenagers stood on the cold and windy street corner. I stopped to talk. We chatted about mobiles, about iPods, about computer games, music and films. But, as our conversation developed, it quickly became clear that what they really wanted to discuss was theology not technology. None of them ever used that term, of course, but the more we talked, the more obvious it became that all their deepest questions were about purpose, meaning and, above all else, hope. Who am I? Where do I fit in? Do I fit in? My dad says I'm an accident – a waste of space – I feel like one most of the time.

But the journey of life is not easy for any of us – our years are filled with tears as well as joy. We are all hungry for meaning; for hope which is as vital to life as food and drink, as essential to our existence as the air we breathe. Starved of it we struggle to survive, let alone flourish and thrive. Hope is not only life-changing, it is life-saving. Indeed, hope is so indispensable to us that those who are gifted with it are capable of astonishing accomplishment and inner strength, whereas those who can't find it – who feel hopeless – are easily crushed, defeated, and tragically, in some cases, even driven to the choice of taking their own lives. Yesterday, I asked someone whom I respect deeply whether they believed it was possible to live without hope. She thought for a moment before replying with simply, 'No, not for long … No'.

I still remember my school days and my all-too-frequent encounters with Mr Jenkins. 'Do your tie up, you nasty little boy. You're a mess, a disgrace. Your mother may love you – that's her problem – but I don't. Stand up straight while I'm talking to you.' To tell you the truth, it was very hard to 'stand up straight' at all, either on the outside or the inside, having been regularly verbally assaulted in this way. None of us are changed by moral exhortation, instead we are transformed by renewed imagination and by the grasping of hope. Individuals, communities and, indeed, whole societies are turned around when their eyes are lifted to see what will be or could be.

In these pages my good friend Nick Baines writes with passion, honesty and accessibility. *Hungry for Hope?* does not skirt or shirk the complexity of the issues life poses. Through it, Nick speaks to us out of both the wisdom of his experience of the pastoral care of others, and a life-time spent seeking Christ through the pain, doubts and questions of his own life. If you are anything like me, you will find that the following pages will challenge you, stimulate you, and bring you hope.

STEVE CHALKE MBE
Founder, Oasis Global

PREFACE

It is probably true that every generation thinks its own world to be on the brink of disaster. It is probably also true that every generation thinks it might be the last. The experience of anyone living in the twenty-first century would seem to give some justification to such a view. Revolutions in Europe in the nineteenth century gave way to a world war which was so horrible that it was thought enough to put off another war for ever. But people have short memories and long prejudices. Revolution in Russia evoked fear in the rest of Europe. The Second World War erupted against a background of fear and oppression. If this was not bloody enough, once the common enemy of Germany had been suppressed, the Allies began their own mutual Cold War. The entire post-war generation has lived with the possibility (which from time to time seemed more like probability) of global thermonuclear war. At the same time as the Cold War was thawing, scientists became increasingly aware of the danger to the planet itself from the lifestyle we have adopted as normal. Just when we seemed to be getting the message home to people in the Western world, the Gulf crises exploded, with oil and Saddam Hussein's head as the major stakes. Terrorism, the plague of HIV/AIDS and climate change all create huge anxieties in some people. Is it any wonder that they cry out for hope?

It is not just at the level of international politics that people perceive the absence of hope. Personal tragedy breaks in to otherwise comfortable lives and evokes a crisis of meaning. Who am I and what am I here for? For a culture that has largely assimilated the deception that science has ousted God from any intelligent worldview, the crisis can be desperate. It comes uninvited and is most unwelcome because it disturbs everything we are and the life we choose to live. Hope is a great casualty of this generation and our Western culture.

This forms the basic reason for writing this book. It is not an academic book aimed at giving a watertight and comprehensive theology of hope. Rather it is an exploration of the theme of hope which is credible and accessible to ordinary people. The book is written with Christians in mind, but it is intended to be a usable account of Christian hope which can also be helpful to those who perceive the absence of hope whilst not having embraced Jesus Christ.

No concern that ends up in book form arises out of a vacuum. This book is no exception. For four years, I worked as a linguist at GCHQ (Government Communications Headquarters) in Cheltenham. Whilst there, I had to explore and understand the politics of a complicated world and know what was going on in that world. This means that I have lived for some time with difficult questions about God's involvement in the world. Such experiences have made me impatient with simplistic Christian world-views, jargon-filled explanations of neat theology which sometimes have little connection with the *real* world. The second impetus for writing this book has been my pastoral experience with individuals who have suffered enormous tragedies. There are times in the life of a pastor when one has to be silent in the face of suffering, simply holding the hand of those who suffer and weeping with them. It is not always appropriate to hand out neatly rounded rational explanations of God's work when someone's world has just fallen apart. It is my hope that this book will be of some help at some point in such people's experience. I hope that it will lead some who despair to find genuine hope in the God who is there.

This book was prompted by my experience with one family in particular, whose tragedy (a suicide) made me think and pray and weep harder than any other. In one sense, this book has been written for Jane.

PREFACE TO THE
REVISED/UPDATED EDITION

This book emerged not from abstract ruminations in a library, but from encounters with ordinary people in an ordinary parish in England. Since its original publication, I have served in several more parishes of different complexions. In 2000, I became Archdeacon of Lambeth, and in May 2003 Bishop of Croydon in the Diocese of Southwark. Work around the world in inter-faith dialogue and ecumenical affairs has broadened my experience and theological thinking, but the substance of what this book represents is basically unchanged.

I still hold to my decision not to quote other books simply in order to prove I have read them. Readers who wish to explore the theology of hope further might wish to read Jürgen Moltmann's seminal *Theology of Hope* (SCM, 1967, reprinted 2002) and Richard Bauckham and Trevor Hart's *Hope Against Hope* (DLT, 1999).

I have resisted the temptation to re-write the book and simply updated and revised those sections that required it. In addition, I have added a new chapter at the beginning of the book. I hope that this small book might be useful to ordinary people who want a simple explanation of hope that resonates with their experience and aspirations.

RT REVD NICK BAINES, June 2007

HOPE FOR A NEW BEGINNING

'Hope' is a word that trips easily off the tongue. It could be said that its currency is diluted by overuse in contexts where something else is intended – 'wishful thinking', for example. But hope is more than a vague aspiration or dream that things might be different.

In April 2007, I led a group to Zimbabwe, where we spent two weeks living, meeting and working with Christians in urban and rural areas. Nothing can prepare you for the experiences that such a visit elicits. This is a country that was once described as 'the breadbasket of Africa', a country of rich resources both in its people and in its environment. Twenty-seven years after Independence from British colonisation, the place is in ruins. Consider the following as a snapshot of how things are in 2007:

- The ravages of HIV/AIDS have reduced life-expectancy for a man to 34 and a woman to 36 years;
- Unemployment is running at 80% in many areas;
- The infrastructure is visibly collapsing, with nothing being repaired or properly maintained;
- Power cuts happen almost every day, and in some places there has been no running water for months;
- Many people are now able to eat only one meal a day, and that will consist simply of rice, maize and a vegetable – little or no meat;
- Many industries have either closed down or are working at a fraction of their capacity;

- The economy is unmanageable and the currency in freefall. Inflation at the time of our visit stood at over 3,500%;
- A severe drought has exacerbated the shortage of basic food resources such as maize, the staple diet;
- The country's brightest professionals have emigrated, leaving shortages of doctors, nurses, teachers and engineers;
- Opposition to or questioning of the ruling elite (Robert Mugabe and his government) invites brutal and violent suppression.

What does it mean to speak of 'hope' to people in this situation? Indeed, one of the problems is that people frequently express the hope that 'things will change', but the conversation dries up when you ask them what they will *do* to bring about that change. For many, 'hope' is simply a desperate wish that God or someone will do something to change their lot in life and make things better. And it is certainly not up to people like me to criticise from a comfortable distance those for whom an appearance above the political parapet might mean a severe beating or worse.

What becomes clear in encounters with such people is that 'hope' works at different levels. Firstly, there is the need for a collective or corporate hope – one that takes account of the wider national and social predicament and keeps alive a vision of how it might one day be shaped differently. Secondly, there is a 'theological' hope that sets current suffering in context and tries to discern the hand of God in both the suffering and the longed-for deliverance from it. But, thirdly, there is a personal or individual hope that might or might not consciously take notice of the first two. Desperate people do not always have the luxury of reading helpful books or intellectually reflecting upon their experience in the light of some theological, economic, political or social theory. Their more immediate question might be: 'Where do I get the next meal from?' or 'Does it matter if I don't see tomorrow?' One clergyman expressed it thus: 'You see us walking, but we are dead already'.

So, a broad and collective theology of hope is vital. But, for many people, the matter is much more personal – individual even – than that. Whether we like it or not, their desire for hope is subjective, immediate and personal. It is to such people that I am addressing this account of Christian hope in this book. Rooted in a biblical theology and appreciation of the world, it nevertheless tries to address the hunger felt by an individual whose world has closed down.

An American theologian, Walter Brueggemann, has explored the role of the Old Testament prophets in keeping hope alive when the world has shut down. Concentrating on the Jews in exile, he describes the challenge to their identity, their understanding of God and their view of the future. What, he asks, is to be said to those who have banked everything on a God who is not a tribal deity but claims to be the creator and sustainer of the whole cosmos, yet now find themselves defeated, abandoned and in exile? The event that gives them their fundamental sense of meaning and identity is the Exodus in which God liberates them from slavery – and here they are, back again under oppression and defeated. How can God be the Creator and Liberator when his people sit on the banks of a foreign power's rivers being mocked by their captors?

Brueggemann's answer is to point to the role of the prophet in keeping hope alive for a people whose world (and worldview) has collapsed. God will not be rushed, and history will have to take its course. But even the seemingly invincible and powerful empires will come to an end, and the future will open up before a people who once felt their definitive end had come. And the role of the prophet in this process? To keep the vision alive whereby the people might one day be enabled to imagine a different world, a different way of being in that world. The prophet is the one who is called upon to see beyond the immediate or the apparent and to hold out what Brueggemann calls a 'hopeful imagination' to a people for whom hope seems more like fantasy.

How is this 'hopeful imagination' to be expressed? Well, says Brueggemann, it won't necessarily be through cleverly articulated rational or philosophical (even theological) arguments. Rather, it is the poets who make this re-imagination of a new future possible. Sometimes we need to put argument and consistent rationality to one side (after all, it only makes you feel even more tired) and listen to the songs, the music, the evocative poetry that reaches deep into our soul and awakens the hope – the possibility – of beauty, of newness, of love, of a future. And, to return to the people of suffering Zimbabwe referred to at the beginning of this chapter, this is one of the roles being enacted by the Christian churches in that beautiful country: they care for the sick, educate the orphans, support the widows, try to feed the hungry, seek to give hope to the fearful and help people to die as well as possible.

The consistent message of the Bible is that human beings are made in the image of God and are, therefore, of infinite value. They live in a temporal and contingent world of time, space and physicality. Where God's people go wrong is when they make fundamental mistakes about God, the world or themselves – for example, in thinking that God is only there when things are going well for us; or that things have gone wrong simply because we have 'sinned'; or that our circumstances are an indicator of God's approval or otherwise. As we shall see in this book, Christian hope for a new future is rooted not in

4

a particular outcome or circumstance, but in a person: God himself. In other words, it is not my escaping illness, suffering or death that gives me hope; but it is the God who raised Jesus of Nazareth from real death that gives hope. That is to say, hope has to be focused on the person of God, not on 'getting my way'.

In one sense, all this comes together in the question: How can this God be trusted – especially where trusting him seems to bring no relief and, indeed, might be the source of the suffering itself? The answer is to be found in the cross and the empty tomb. God is not a mere theoretical philosopher, content to knock around ideas and observe the world from a distance. As the prologue to the fourth Gospel puts it, 'the Word' did not remain an 'idea', but took flesh and lived among us. He has been here and knows the reality of physicality and all that comes with mortality. Resurrection is not about Jesus' molecules reassembling in a tomb; it is (as the Apostle Paul recognised) about 'God raised Christ from the dead'. Christian hope that is to have any meaning has to be rooted in a person, not in an outcome that satisfies the cry of a particular mind, body or soul.

But this is to pre-empt the journey this book is intended to take us on and to strike ahead of the contours of the land we will traverse. However, it is probably useful to set out concisely at the beginning the general direction in which we will travel – a sort of compass for the meanderings of the future.

2

WHATEVER HAPPENED
TO HOPE?

Like most adolescents, to be told that I was 'hopeless' was not a very encouraging experience. I can well remember the occasion when a schoolteacher, having just seen my latest efforts at understanding algebra, pronounced that severe judgement on my young head. Of course, the teacher was not suggesting I end my life there and then. Knowing I had strengths in areas other than mathematics, he was merely using the word 'hopeless' rather loosely. He knew that I had a future somewhere, but that the somewhere would have to be reasonably independent of numbers.

However, to call someone genuinely 'hopeless' is to pass a dreadful sentence. For someone who is hopeless is literally someone who has no hope. And someone who has no hope is someone who has no future. To have no future is to be condemned to live and relive the past. Hopelessness is wedded to a lack of vision, an absence of meaning and purpose. To be truly hopeless is to despair; for life then holds nothing of lasting value, and the prospects for meaningful life are bleak indeed.

In 1974, the great Bishop Lesslie Newbigin returned to England after serving the Church in South India for nearly forty years. Back in his 'home' country, he was frequently asked to identify his greatest difficulty in moving back from a developing (Eastern) to a developed (Western) culture. He always answered: 'The disappearance of hope'.[1] In contrast to other 'less developed' cultures in the world, the affluent and self-confident Europe appeared to have lost its hope. It was now trapped in a cynicism of its own making. It had lost its meaning and purpose. Newbigin died before he had to witness the embarrassment in the European Union at any reference to Christianity in accounting for the history of the continent. The collapse of Communism and the expansion of Europe brought hope to millions, but were followed by new forms of Islamic terrorism and subsequent ill-conceived wars in the Middle East.

There are many reasons why hope can seem to be in short supply. This situation has not happened overnight, but has crept up on us like a slow death. Cultural cynicism is like gangrene: it eats away until it starves the body of life. Inevitably, brevity and generalisation raise certain questions, and the picture can never be as simple as it might at first appear. But there have been very significant shifts in the ways in which we think about and see the world. A brief and generalised historical sketch will help us understand something of what has happened in what used to be called 'the West'.

THE DETHRONEMENT OF GOD

Up until the eighteenth century, God had an assured place in the framework by which people in Europe understood the world. The assumed fact of God's existence profoundly affected, if not directed, people's understanding of themselves and their experiences. God was the lens through which people looked at life and gave it meaning. Theology was very much the Queen of the Sciences.

Then a very significant shift began to occur. Thinkers and artists began seriously to question God's existence. They began to explore ways of looking at life and the world without bringing God into the picture. For them, God's existence became increasingly irrelevant to real life. We do not need God, they said, so let's kill him off. After all, even if we do kill him off, or just ignore him, we will still wake up tomorrow and the world will keep turning. God makes no difference. Humanity is the only god that matters, and we are answerable only to ourselves. Human beings are responsible for creating their own little world and giving it meaning. We ought to grow up and take responsibility for ourselves; after all, we are simply random bits of genetic 'stuff' and owe no duty (in an inherently meaningless world) to anyone but ourselves.

This discarding of God and the supernatural became known as the 'Enlightenment'. The light of reason was displacing the superstition of religious belief. Humanity was finally coming of age.[2]

Now, despite this concise caricature of the Enlightenment, it also achieved much that was good and helpful. It sounded the death-knell of a good deal of iniquitous religious superstition and ultimately forced a complacent Christian Church to wake up. The challenge to the very roots of its beliefs and role in society had to be met. But a long-term effect of the Enlightenment was gradually to remove God from the real world of human joy and pain, decision-making and morality. The universe became viewed as closed to God's interest or interference. Religion became privatised in the minds of individuals, the spiritual being seen as an optional extra for the emotionally lame and afflicted. Belief in God was seen as a matter of individual taste. One was free to believe; but it must be kept private.

In the following two centuries, despite religious fashions and revivals, this humanistic view of the world took a strong hold on political and economic institutions and policymaking structures. Any talk of God was not allowable in the issues of the real world. God was to be reserved for church. And the Church was dissuaded from attempting to involve itself in spheres of life and society which were not its proper concern. This privatised religion could have little cutting edge to it. It is as virile as a eunuch. And the tragedy is that, in many places, the Church happily colluded in its own neutering. The situation largely persists today, although the signs of fertility are increasing.[3]

THE ENTHRONEMENT OF SCIENCE

As God was being ousted as a relevant factor in real life, so human confidence in our own liberty, independence and technological cleverness blossomed. Science – the search for *how* the world works, rather than *why* it is as it is – came to replace theology as the framework for understanding life and the universe. The mechanical questions of 'how' and 'when' replaced the 'why' of exploration and meaning. The spiritual became a mere extra to the essentials of mind and body. For science can only deal with what can be seen, touched, smelled and quantified. And this deification of science still dominates the public discourse, despite the flowering of a million 'spiritualities' and therapies.

In fact, this dichotomy between science and faith is, and always was, a false and unnecessary one. For science and religion have different functions in accounting for the one reality. However, generations of popular distinction have created a contemporary situation in which the assumption of conflict between the two is very difficult to dispel.[4]

Suffice it to say, however, human cleverness knew no bounds. The countless benefits of technological progress changed life throughout the world. Yet along with the benefits came the horrors of technological evil. Within the short space of twenty or so years, humanity had 'progressed' from a one-man aeroplane flight of several yards to sophisticated methods of airborne bombing. And that was only the First World War, the so-called 'war to end all wars'. Within another twenty-five years, entire cities were being destroyed and their populations exterminated. Sophisticated technological cruelty knew few limits. Human beings had begun to achieve their potential as self-determining gods, grasping the belief that power could be won using the tools of science and technology. Yet this new idol was growing up into an uncontrollable and rebellious teenager with a mind of his own.

THE DARK SIDE OF THE ENLIGHTENMENT

As technology opened up a bright new future, full of hitherto unimagined possibilities, so people became increasingly disillusioned with the seeming human propensity to turn such cleverness to appalling use. Two world wars shattered the illusion of human pseudo-deity. Even if the technology was essentially neutral, morality certainly was not. The great scientific maxim seemed to be: *If it is possible, it must be legitimate.* Morality could only drag along behind, often unable to cope with the journey.

In the second half of the twentieth century, the world became increasingly small and complex, and life became increasingly dangerous and bewildering. The prospect of annihilation became very real, be it through global nuclear war or disastrous environmental pollution.[5] The irony that we could put a man on the moon, admiring the beauty of the earth from thousands of miles in space, whilst still being unable to live peacefully together on the earth, was not lost.

The twentieth century saw such horror and inhumanity walking hand in hand with clever exploitation of imagination and technological resources that disillusionment grew in many quarters. Life certainly became more convenient and comfortable for many people, and the possibility of enormous wealth became achievable for some. Some nations are very rich and powerful, failing to

10

see that their gain and comfort come at enormous cost to others. The fall of oppressive Communism brought unprecedented optimism in Europe, only to see it wiped out in a decade by new forms of militancy and terrorism that brought down icons of capitalist and materialist power: the Twin Towers of New York City on 11 September 2001.

The end of the Second World War saw the liberation of concentration camps and exposure of Hitler's Final Solution to 'the Jewish problem'. Never again could human beings get away with such horror. Well, sixty years later and Bosnia, Rwanda and Darfur (just to cite a few) remind us that our resolve is not as firm as we would like to think – that the challenges of the twentieth century have not disappeared with the emerging complexities of the twenty-first. Climate change and environmental degradation now dominate the headlines as we wonder how to reverse the trends and ways of life engendered by our wonderful technological expertise and inventiveness.

FLICKERING LIGHTS

Along with the horror stories, however, there have also been periodic revivals of hope and compassion, a temporary (and sometimes fashionable) rebellion against the materialist values of our society. For example, we should not forget just how the extraordinary 'Band Aid' and 'Live Aid' phenomena of 1985 powerfully captured the world's imagination. The straggling figure of Bob Geldof, a pop singer, doing what politicians did not have the vision or humanity to do, encouraged millions to hope once again. It was confirmation that things do not have to stay as they are; even individuals of vision can change the world.

Countless examples of self-sacrifice for the sake of the world's poor make for heartening reading and listening.

Care for those who have been ravaged by HIV/AIDS continues to be costly, but has changed the way disastrous illness is tackled in a moralising world. As time moves on and things change, optimism grows and wanes. The fall of the Berlin Wall heralded the collapse of the Soviet Empire. But a decade later and cynicism was rife in parts of Eastern Europe where unemployment was higher than ever, prospects had not brightened in the new world order, and disillusionment had begun to set in again.

There is a potential problem here. Optimism can cloud reality and hinder a proper and reasonable appreciation of what is happening. The euphoria in Europe did not easily entertain the caution of those who saw danger in the new-found liberties. All the institutions and old securities fell away as the race to fill the vacuum left behind began. Instant solutions, though desirable, proved to be illusory. Freedom of itself was worth nothing – a hard realisation for some. Optimism needed to be tempered by realism. Otherwise, genuine hope became swallowed up by wishful thinking.

THE BANKRUPTCY OF MATERIALISM

One of the most significant paradoxes of the latter half of the twentieth and the beginning of the twenty-first centuries is that powerful materialism and technological prowess, so eagerly sought after for so long, have led simultaneously to a growing dissatisfaction with the purely material. The 1960s celebrated permissiveness to the point of licence; and thousands trekked off to India to seek someone or something to quench their spiritual thirst. The 1970s saw near economic disaster in some Western countries – and with it a growing thirst for spiritual reality. The religion of self-fulfilment found a ready market among people who have material comfort and still feel empty. The 1980s saw a dramatic explosion of environmental consciousness; the earth and the self became gods for the New Age generation. The 1990s saw political earthquakes in Europe and mass migration over newly fallen borders in search of a better life. The 2000s have seen religion dominating world politics and economics to the complete surprise (and chagrin) of the liberal elite who thought religion was dead, buried and irrelevant to the modern world.

This very real yearning for spiritual reality in a material world has shown itself in many different ways. For example, it pushed the churches to the forefront of Eastern European revolution. Interest in the occult and witchcraft has accompanied a flourishing trade in astrology. The various offspring of the New Age movement had a powerful appeal because they enabled us to worship a visible god, a hybrid of self-realisation in harmony with nature. In reality they are a bizarre mixture of convenient beliefs, according to which we can create God in our own image and see him in everything. 'New Age' thinking is a sort of materialist pantheism, and, though riddled with contradiction, it is very attractive to many people.

It is not surprising that this enormous growth in spiritual/religious interest has gone hand in hand with burgeoning material prosperity and scientific understanding in Europe. The technological world we have created and attempted to master has only helped us to understand some of the mechanics of the world. It has not helped us one iota in the spiritual search for a real answer to life's most pressing question: *Why am I here?* The truth is that our culture confronts a crisis of meaning, and science of itself has no answer to offer. Scientific materialism can only maintain a disinterested silence in the face of the screams of millions of victims of the Hitlers, Stalins, Pol Pots and Saddams of this world. It is not in the least bit surprising that despair and a sense of pointless nihilism in the affluent and materialist world evoke a thirsty longing for spiritual reality that will make life meaningful. That is surely what we were created for in the first place.

THE GREAT IDOL

As indicated above, one interesting aspect of contemporary social, political and ethical thought is the shift from the assumption of duty and responsibility to that of self-fulfilment. If I am feeling frustrated within my marriage, if my ambitions are not realising their full potential, if I am inhibited by the needs or claims of others, then I ought to release myself from this cage. Nothing is to get in the way of my being fulfilled. It is caught up inevitably with the success mentality of a culture which has come to believe that one's goal in life is to *achieve*. The concept of service, of losing one's life for the sake of others, does not meet with an enthusiastic welcome in a world that reveres beauty, success and possession of a particular 'image'. Just look at the values represented (or betrayed) on the front covers of a random selection of glossy magazines in any supermarket.

This selfishness is the god of our culture. It is a very convenient god, because it is made in our own image and it never says 'You're wrong'. It is a fundamental under-standing of life which pervades much popular modern theology and makes its adherents worship idols: the dramatic, the successful, the attractive, the powerful. It has within it the seeds of its own destruction, however. For these values are transient, dissatisfying in the long term, and destructive of relationships and even self-respect. We are not created purely to be served; we are created to serve. And that is a difficult concept, which contradicts worship of the idol: that we actually find life when we lose it; that we are most fulfilled when we die to self.[6]

THE RECOVERY OF HOPE

It is nothing short of a tragedy that so many people searching for spiritual reality should ignore the Church of Jesus Christ. In many ways, the institutional churches are widely rejected as sources of spiritual nourishment. It is even more tragic that the message of Jesus Christ should be rejected without having been heard or properly understood. Instead of being a sign of the Kingdom of God, the Church is often perceived as a pale reflection of the values and experiences of the world, offering nothing other than conflict, self-righteousness and self-importance. The bad news is that many people do not even get as far as considering the Good News of Jesus.

One of the reasons for this state of affairs (and no doubt there are many) is the acquiescence of the Church in allowing faith to be privatised, not letting it impinge too greatly on other areas of life. For to let faith in Jesus loose in the real world of politics, finance, leisure, sex and so on might not be a very tidy affair. As we shall see later, God, by donning flesh and bones and living among us as one of us, has something very direct to say about privatised faith.

Christians also are not exempt from the crisis of meaning we have been describing thus far. Sometimes their lifestyle and anxieties do not sit easily with their professed faith. For example, there are many Christians who might be termed 'activists'. They claim absolute assurance of God's love and their personal salvation. They claim to be saved by God's grace alone. Yet in practice they seem to justify themselves to God by the amount they can do for him. They go to meetings and feel guilty about all the things they do not do for God. They are constantly trying to be better for God. In fact their activism is their enemy. Frequently the bubble bursts, they experience doubts and

15

they feel even more guilty. The stakes are too high for them to admit to serious doubt or crisis. What they have lost is actually their source of hope. They face a crisis of meaning and have to choose whether to risk losing face in the Church by addressing their predicament seriously and honestly, or to hide behind false hopes (that God will reward their activism by magically and dramatically making them all right) and thus avoid the issue.

For many Christians, the reality of their crisis has profound implications. This whole matter of coping with the spiritual desert will be discussed in a later chapter, but it is important to remember at this point that Christians also can have their experience of hopelessness and crisis.

We all need to find hope. Meaning and hope are inextricably intertwined. People who have lost sight of God and meaning for their lives, not necessarily knowingly or willingly, have often also lost hope. For Christian hope points towards and anticipates a future. It rests on a fundamental conviction that life and death are meaningful. It is rooted in the assurance that this meaning can be grasped and understood. Its fruit is a radically changed life and lifestyle. It believes that things do not have to be the way they are, that change is possible and necessary. History is not random or aimless; it is purposeful, and God is not simply a disinterested observer.

HOPE: PERSONAL BUT NOT PRIVATE

Our analysis so far has painted a very broad picture, using global events by way of illustration. But we have begun to move on to the experience of hope and hopelessness at a more personal level. It is this, and the implications of it, which form the concern of this particular book. The question about hope for the world or humanity in general can be passed over or answered generally. The question about my own source of hope for the past, present and future hits closer to home. It is much more difficult to ignore.

I once knew a young woman who was bereaved in tragic circumstances. She developed a thirst to know, and to know about God. She began to ask all her friends what they believed and how and why they believed it. This made people feel very uncomfortable. Normally, other people do not ask such awkward and personal questions so persistently. They knew that any old answer would not do. But the questions were serious and could not be avoided. Several people discovered that they did not know what they believed about God (or life), why they believed it, or how they had come to believe it in the first place. This, I suggest, is not a rare experience.

When something happens to strip life of its thin veneer of trivial respectability, it is easy to feel lost and uncomfortable. We feel very vulnerable. The easiest thing to do is keep the shutters up and not let anyone come too close. But that is to foster false hopes and to court disaster. The courageous response is to face reality, with all its implications of weakness and failure, and confront the difficult questions.

The most important question is that of identity: who exactly am I? Am I just a random collection of chemicals, collected in cells and motivated by electrical impulses in my brain? Do I give my own life meaning, however arbitrary, or do I have any inherent value as a human being? Do I actually matter? It is the inability to cope confidently with such questions which can lead to despair. If I do not matter, why continue to live? If life is simply a charade, random and without meaning, why bother to undergo such strain and suffering? If I do not matter and have no inherent value, than neither does anybody else. I can legitimately be a totally selfish individual.

This is why Christians maintain that it is important for value to be attributed objectively, that is, from outside of ourselves. Subjective self-value is inadequate and can be somewhat arbitrary. To conclude that I matter, that I have inherent value as a human being because God created me and loves me, is to discover the source of genuine hope. God thinks I matter. God thinks my life, with all its frailty, is important and valuable. This simple fact changes my life, my relationships and my whole view of the world.

THE SHATTERING OF FALSE HOPES

However, before proceeding to put some flesh on the skeleton of hope, it is first essential to dispel the illusions of false hopes. For it is these that prevent us from facing the real dilemma cited above: who am I, and does it matter?

It is our false hopes which fill our lives with disillusionment and disappointment. I might hope that my submarine will fly at high altitude. All the faith in the world will not prevent my frustration and grief. I might live with the illusion of its possibility for many years, but if that hope is ever tested it will be found wanting. In the context of biblical history, Stephen Travis comments: 'The crashing of false hopes becomes the Lord's way of pointing his people to a fresh beginning. Until false hopes are put aside, there is no chance for real hopes to be grasped.'[7] False hopes are to be recognised, acknowledged for what they really are, and replaced by a genuine source of hope which will not be disappointed.

Perhaps, then, the first task of evangelism is to dispel false hopes. Before you can recognise the Good News of Jesus Christ, you need to recognise the bad news of your current position. A message of hope is not going to impress someone who does not recognise hopelessness or an absence of purpose. Both inside and outside the Church, there is a vital need to face reality and to cease hiding behind the comfortable walls of our tamed illusions, however secure and righteous they make us feel.

In his book *The Meaning of the City*,[8] the French theologian, Jacques Ellul, describes the story of Cain in the Old Testament. In Genesis 4, we read that Cain was jealous of his brother, Abel. In a fit of rage, Cain killed Abel and, like his parents before him, discovered he was answerable to a consistent and just God. Cain's selfish disregard of his brother's worth demanded a just response, and he was sent away to construct a new life.

Interestingly, the story relates how Cain left God behind and chose to live life without reference to God. He was to live as if God did not exist (although God had placed his mark of protection on him). Cain, we read, built a city and called it Enoch. Why, asks Ellul, did Cain build a city? And why should this detail be recorded in the Genesis narrative?

By way of reply, he suggests that what Cain did is simply an accurate picture of what everyone does. When we leave God out and live life without reference to him, we are forced to create our own world which will give us both meaning and security, a sense of belonging somewhere. The walls of our city provide us with a framework for understanding where we fit into the world. Often our efforts at constructing the high walls of our city occupy our minds and affections, thus preventing us from recalling or recognising what we have lost. We busy ourselves to death in an attempt to find or create meaning without addressing the difficult questions cited earlier. These walls, which are supposed to afford us security, in fact become the barrier which blocks out the genuine source of light: God himself.

Those cities whose walls collapse amid the invasion of reality or despair might well be seen as the most fortunate ones. Such a rude awakening often comes painfully through

19

tragedy and suffering. When the walls come down, it is at least possible once again to see the sun. When we see the surrounding countryside, it helps put our own little city in a certain perspective. The real tragedy is that all too often new walls are quickly erected to replace the old ones. The light proves too disturbing, too revealing, too threatening; and we prefer the security of walled darkness.[9]

I once met a man in the centre of the UK city of Bristol who was readily engaged in conversation. He deplored the state of the world, the sheer inhumanity of many people and powers, the evil exploitation of technology, and even the gross immorality (as he put it) of the weapons development industry, from which he had only recently retired. He described all this at great length as I listened. I eventually mentioned the Bible's diagnosis of what has gone wrong. On mention of the word 'sin', the man interrupted, declaring with confidence that he was sure humanity is capable of sorting out the mess and creating a peaceful and just world. To reach this conclusion after rehearsing at such length the tragic and consistent failure of human beings through history was more than a little surprising. He would not talk about God or Jesus Christ. His mind was made up, his city walls in place, and argument or evidence was not going to be allowed to disturb them. <u>False hopes can be very firmly embedded and very difficult to uproot.</u>

HUNGRY FOR HOPE

People are always hungry for hope, for a vision that will help them imagine and create a better and more meaningful world for themselves and their children. Many people fear for the present, to say nothing of the future. Our children live with the fear of violence, disease and ecological catastrophe. Terrorism strikes closer to home than we would like to admit. People are hungry for reality, thirsty for a sense of meaning and peace.

When the future is insecure or frightening, the need for hope is extremely powerful. When we have all we need materially, but life seems somehow empty, we search for significance. When the routine and pressures of everyday life cause us to question what it is all for, we thirst and hunger for hope. We cry out for someone or something to assure us that we matter, that our lives do not have to be hopeless or aimless. We cry out for value and love. We crave a sense of grounded peace in heart and mind. We long for an answer to the question 'why?' Like the writer of Psalm 42, 'my soul thirsts for God, for the living God'. It takes enormous courage to admit our predicament. But we do not rest until we have found him.

A HISTORY OF HOPE

A speaker at a Christian house party paused to tell a story. He was offering an example of how some Christians have the most bizarre understandings of how God guides us. According to the story, a young student had fallen in love with a girl on his campus. He prayed fervently about whether he ought to ask her to marry him. One day, he decided to put God to the test. In this way, God's guidance would be unambiguously understood. He prayed that, if it were God's will that he should marry this girl, he should come across the words 'chilli con carne' during that day. At lunchtime, he went over to the refectory and discovered to his utter amazement that on the menu that day was ... chilli con carne! Staggered at God's clear guidance, he prayed even more fervently, before going to see the girl in question.

At this point, the speaker paused to allow the laughter to subside. Then he made the story even funnier by telling us that the girl had never spoken to the man and did not even know him! This extra knowledge changed the nature of the story and its impact on the audience. After the laughter had subsided once more, he surprised everyone with the news that the two students actually did start going out together and eventually got married. This turn of events had not been expected by the audience, and, like the punchline of any good joke, evoked near-hysteria. But that was still not the end of the story. As the laughter died down, the speaker told us that they were now divorced.

There was muted but spontaneous laughter at this new twist in the tale, followed by an embarrassed silence. We knew that we had responded inappropriately at each point in the story because we did not know the end until we got there.

The reason for relating this story is that the speaker could have finished at any point. We might have thought the student was silly for testing God's will in such a ridiculous way and would deserve to be rebuffed by the girl. After all, what sort of girl would take seriously an unknown man asking her to marry him on the basis that God had made chilli con carne appear on the refectory menu? However, the additional news that in fact they *had* got married completely changed the story and altered our understanding of why the speaker was telling it. He had caught us out. Perhaps the student was actually more spiritually aware than we were. As God is a God of surprises, perhaps we ought not to be so cynical.

The final punchline, that the couple had now divorced, completely changed the meaning of the story, the message to be drawn from it, and the reason for the speaker relating it to us in the first place. If the speaker had stopped the story at an earlier stage, he might have made a quite legitimate point to illustrate his theme. Had he done so, however, we would not have fully understood the story. The implications we might have drawn from it would have been incomplete and founded on a selective history. Our judgements would have been faulty and unreliable because the evidence they were based on was inadequate and incomplete. We would have been deceived.

The analogy with history is obvious. It is impossible to understand history properly without knowing its end. The ending of a story gives meaning to the total ingredients of it. Judgements made in the course of the story can be confounded by the turn of events at the end. This is the

23

principle behind some good novels, exciting thrillers or gripping television serials. And this introduces us to the essential paradox of history: the future gives meaning to the past, but an understanding of the past is essential for having a *reasonable* hope for the future. This is what T. S. Eliot is describing when he writes:

> Time present and time past
> Are both perhaps present in time future,
> And time future contained in time past.[1]

THE END OF HISTORY

The immediate response of many people to the assertion that the end of history must be known if the past is to be understood is to look amazed. How, they wonder, can we possibly know the future? It is impossible to guarantee what will happen in the next five minutes, let alone discover the ultimate meaning of the universe at the end of time! However, it is the bold and confident assertion of Christian faith that to claim such knowledge is neither arrogant nor fantastic, but both reasonable and necessary.

Wolfhart Pannenberg, a German theologian, has made this the linchpin of his theological understanding. He affirms that God reveals himself. History is the sphere of his self-revelation, for it is in historical *events and developments* that we encounter the God who acts. A God who acts in history can never be treated simply as an interesting concept.[2] But God's self-revelation cannot be real or complete if it is seen in any isolated bit of history. History must be completed, and God's revelation of himself must be discovered at the end of history. Only then can history be viewed as a whole. Pannenberg answers the objection we raised in the previous paragraph by stating that in Jesus Christ, and particularly in his resurrection, the end of history has been made known.[3] The resurrection of Jesus is effectively the end time brought forward and invading history, a sort of foretaste of the nature of the consummation of history. It is the point when the King takes full possession of his kingdom.[4]

Whereas there is much to be debated in Pannenberg's theology and understanding, this view of the end giving meaning to the past is very helpful to us. It means that a judgement has to be made about the history of God's dealings with his world. It demands, most importantly, that we come off the fence and make a judgement about Jesus: *Is* he the one he claims to be? *Is* the incarnation the pivotal point in human history? *Is* his resurrection cosmically significant? Is history *really* going anywhere? The answer we give to these questions and the consequent commitment we make will change our lives. For they are not trivial or merely academic, theoretical questions. They demand a response in the sphere of values, priorities, lifestyle, spirituality, commitment and behaviour.

The Bible is a record of God's acts in history and his dealings with people, communities and nations. It provides a God-centred (theological) interpretation of historical events and developments. In the Bible, we find a coherent view of a history that has purpose and meaning. The future is unknown in detail, but the risen Christ will see his kingdom of justice and righteousness established – probably much to the surprise of many people who have already worked out his timetable and itinerary until the end of the world as we know it. This future can be grasped by faith. But, as the writer(s) to the Hebrews says, 'faith is being sure of what we hope for and certain of what we do not see' (Hebrews 11:1). It is a reasonable hope because it is founded on a reasonable commitment to the person of Jesus. It is a hope which stands or falls on the resurrection of Jesus and his claim to cosmic authority.[5]

It would be easy at this point to enter a long philosophical or theological discussion of the nature or reasonableness of Christian hope. I suspect that most readers would give up and turn to something more directly helpful to their own experience of hope or despair. Therefore, although the issues demand proper treatment, I must leave that to other writers with other agendas. Suffice it to say for the present issue that every human being has a framework of hope (a worldview) which gives meaning to their lives. Everyone makes an (albeit often unconscious) assumption about what ultimately matters, of how the future might vindicate the past and present. The hope we are talking about in this book is not an airy-fairy, otherworldly, irrational fantasy. Rather it is a hope which, although not exempting us from suffering, doubt or confusion, does help explain or account for our experience and history. And this has personal and social aspects to it.

Whereas definitions can be helpful and, if pithy, memorable, it is more often pictures or illustrations which make more sense to many people. Such stories appeal to the imagination and are easy to identify with. And so, we can now proceed to an account of experiences of hope. These will be taken from the Bible, which is a book full of stories[6] and will serve to show how hope motivates people and leads them into the future. It will reveal how one person's (or nation's) hope can be perverted and become another's tyranny. Yet it will also show how the root of that genuine hope, founded on faith in and experience of God, both encourages and challenges those who hold to it. Hope can sometimes be most inconvenient and extremely uncomfortable.

IN THE BEGINNING ...

The early chapters of Genesis are concerned with answering the question 'why?' rather than the question 'how?' That is to say, they are accounting for the existence and meaning of humanity, and not simply providing a scientific or chronological schedule for the origins of the universe. The point is that creation was not simply a series of random accidents, but had purpose and design. According to Genesis 1, God is pleased with every aspect of his creation, which is ideal and has integrity, each aspect of the created order existing harmoniously. Then the pinnacle of creation is reached with the genesis of humanity:

> So God created man
>   in his own image,
> in the image of God
>   he created him;
> male and female
>   he created them.[7]

The unity of creation depends on human beings. They are here in order to care for the world of which they have been made stewards.[8] This fact has many implications. Human beings are clearly created as complex beings: they are *physical* beings, in harmony with their environment; they are *spiritual* beings, enjoying unity of purpose in their relationship with their creator; they are made for relationships (with God, other people and creation); they are *emotional* beings, capable of loving, appreciating beauty and complementarity, worshipping, recreating, cultivating; and they are *rational* beings, designed to reason, understand and exercise moral choice. All of this is held together within a framework of a purposeful relationship between the creator God and the created humanity. There was an essential integrity in God's design.

The story of the Fall vividly portrays what has happened to God's creation. People decide to go their own way, preferring to see themselves as autonomous rather than contingent. They try to exceed his order in creation, and the potential bearers of a crown gamble it away with impunity. Helmut Thielicke describes the human dilemma as follows:

> What makes [man] the image of God is his character as a *person*, that is, the fact that he is responsible to God ... God put his ordained purpose into every living creature ... Man has the responsible task of *realizing* his created structure, his divine determination, and ... he can fail to do this. The shepherd dog is not confronted with the decision whether it is going to be a shepherd dog; but man does have to decide whether he wills to realize his determination as a man, as a child of God. And because he is faced with this decision, he can decide otherwise.[9]

The Genesis account of the Fall describes the reality which we experience daily, and which leads many to utter despair. Adam and Eve's instinct is to hide from God, as if it were possible to do so. The consequences of their misplaced pride are far-reaching: disintegration, fear, shame, fragmentation, unwillingness to shoulder responsibility when face to face with God. As Mark Twain has observed, 'Man is the only animal that blushes. Or needs to.'

It can be said that the end of history is here established in its very beginning. The end of history is, as Paul puts it, to reconcile all things to God.[10] The disintegration will be reversed, and harmony will once more be established. The image of God in humanity will no longer be scarred and defaced. This will not happen by magic, but will be worked out as history progresses towards the decisive event of God's consummation. Of course, at the time Genesis was written, the detail was unknown. But there was the conviction that creation was not random, that life was meaningful, that history was going somewhere, that the mess we humans make need not be the end of the story. In short, there is hope.

This understanding of the world is fundamental to all that follows in the Bible. Historical events and developments are seen as significant in so far as they point the way towards a time when God's original purposes for the whole created order would be fulfilled. And that is the end time, rooted and prefigured in the beginning time, and giving meaning to the in-between times. And it is the story of those in-between times, as depicted in the Bible, to which we shall now turn.

A BRIEF HISTORY OF ISRAEL

The story goes something like this. God chose a particular people to be a living demonstration – an incarnation, if you like – of his character and purposes for the rest of the world. In the Genesis narrative, he makes covenants with his people which guarantee their future. However, these guarantees are dependent on certain conditions, that the people also live for the fulfilment of God's purposes. We shall look briefly at these covenants.

Noah: 'Never again will all life be cut off by the waters of a flood; never again will there be a flood to destroy the earth' (Genesis 9:11). In fact, this covenant is made with all living creatures, not just humanity. Its force is to promise that however appearances might point to the contrary, God will not allow his creation to be obliterated. Therefore, even if our situation becomes dire, we are assured that God is not asleep, that justice will be done, that his purposes will not ultimately be frustrated. However deep and damp one's personal, social or national quagmire might be, it will not turn into an eternal and annihilating flood. For God has promised a purposeful future. Incidentally, a further implication of this is that our death, which is inevitable, must be inherently meaningful and need not be fearful.[11]

29

Abraham: God's covenant with Abraham appeared to be utterly ridiculous. In Genesis 12:2 and 17:1–22, he promised Abram (as he was then known) the blessing of land, posterity and a relationship with himself that was to have enormous implications. The problem, which was not lost on Abraham, was his wife's infertility. The promise to Abraham and elderly Sarah depended on her having a baby, and the prospect looked worse than impossible. No wonder Sarah laughed (Genesis 18:12) when she heard she was to enjoy sex again and give birth. Within the year, she had delivered a son (Genesis 21) and she was laughing on the other side of her face. It was as if God was showing that his purposes *will* be fulfilled, whatever apparent obstacles we perceive.

However, Abraham and Sarah did not find life easy or straightforward from this point on. The fact that they had received God's promise and that God had proved himself to them irrefutably did not mean that their lives became simple, with every problem resolved. They were not perfect people. They suffered family problems and dramatic bereavement (Genesis 18 and 19), they got into dreadful predicaments because of their fears and the lies they told (Genesis 20), their faith was tested to breaking point (Genesis 22), Abraham was widowed (Genesis 23) and had problems getting his son married off (Genesis 24). God had made his promises and he was working them out in the real world with real people. Abraham was not a superman; but, all in all, he trusted that God was not just playing around with him. The conviction that his life was purposeful burned within him. That was at the heart of his hope.

Moses: Abraham's son, Isaac, had two sons by his wife, Rebekah. One of them, Jacob, deceived his father and received the blessing rightfully owed to his twin brother, Esau. The history of God's chosen people is not illustrious. These are marvellously and recognisably real people, and their story can be read in the remainder of Genesis. Jacob had a large family and spoiled his second-youngest son, Joseph. Joseph's arrogance inflamed the jealousy of his older brothers, and they conspired to sell him into slavery. The plan worked (Genesis 37), but later apparently backfired. For, although sold into slavery in Egypt, Joseph rose to become the king's Chief Executive or Prime Minister. When famine struck Canaan, Joseph's brothers (and eventually his father, now called Israel) migrated to Egypt, where they were reconciled with Joseph.

Israel's people obeyed the command to 'go forth and multiply' and eventually evolved into a powerful minority immigrant community. The Egyptians began to see them as a threat and started to abuse and persecute them. Plus ça change. It must have made the Israelites question the efficacy of God's promises and covenants. In the midst of persecution, how were they to understand God's promise of blessing?

Out of this unpromising and endlessly painful situation emerged a leader of dubious qualities. Moses was more Egyptian than most Israelites, having been brought up and educated in the king's household. He was a murderer. He later had a very clear encounter with God[12] and received his commission to be the liberator of the Israelite people. What a privilege for a man uniquely placed to perform the delicate task of diplomacy and negotiation. Unfortunately, Moses did not see it as a privilege. He wriggled and wriggled to try to get out of it, pleading everything short of diminished responsibility or insanity before reluctantly agreeing to go along with it. His brother, who later proved himself to be somewhat irresolute as a leader, was to help him out.

This unlikely pair mediated between God, the Egyptian king and the Israelite community. Their liberation, when it came, was dramatic[13] and violent. They rejoiced that their hope, however wavering in the recent past, had been vindicated – that God had not forgotten them after all. But the next forty years of learning to trust God in the wilderness sorely tested their understanding of God's dealings with them. God established a conditional covenant with them at Sinai,[14] a covenant which was to shape and order their relationships with God and with each other. Running through this (as well as the earlier covenants with Noah and Abraham) is God's essential justice. He will not be mocked and his purposes will not ultimately be frustrated. He *will* establish justice and *will* unite all things under him in the end.

After the tortuous experiences of the desert, Israel did eventually enter the Promised Land. But this was not the end of the story. Battles had to be fought there, defeats had to be survived and tests had to be faced. The emerging nation had to establish political, economic and judicial order based on God's clear command for integrity, justice and God-centred love. The subsequent history of monarchy, with its successes and disasters, can be followed in the remaining books of the Pentateuch[15] and into the history books of the Old Testament. But, as even a cursory reading demonstrates, it is not a very glorious history, despite David and Solomon. But it is the history of God's dealings with his people. And it is the history of their vacillating hope in his promise that their story would eventually have a proper and just ending.

David and Solomon: In 2 Samuel 7, God makes a covenant with David. He promises that despite his son Solomon's successes and failures as king, his kingdom will be established for ever. In verse 14, it is made clear that Solomon will face the consequences of his mistakes. God will not intervene supernaturally to punish or correct him; rather, he will be punished by real people in the real world using real means. However, it is obvious that either God did not fulfil his promises, or that we are to understand the Davidic throne in a different way. God is not promising that there will be an eternal succession of successful kings of Israel, but rather that the *nature* of Israel's kingship – reflecting the character of God himself – is to continue, whatever the particular historical circumstances Israel encounters and whatever forms of authority they enjoy or endure. The leaders of the people are to represent the character of God in the way they govern the people. This, of course, is the time when the idea of a messianic hope began to take root.

As a footnote to this, and as a hint of what will be discussed in Chapter 4 of this book, it is worth reinforcing the observation that God has made his covenants with ordinary human people. David and Solomon were not superheroes, nor were Moses or Abraham. Like the disciples of Jesus, they were people living in the real world, full of weakness and limited vision; people who trusted that God could do something with them despite their obvious faults and frailties.

The Prophets: After Solomon, the kingdom divided between Israel in the north and Judah in the south. Eventually, Israel and Samaria succumbed to the onslaught of the Assyrian empire in 722 BCE, and Israel ceased to exist as a separate nation. She went into exile, thus losing the land and thereby the physical guarantee of God's blessing. Judah survived until 587 BCE, when she was conquered by the Babylonians. These abject defeats and the consequent exiles should not have come as a surprise. There had been a stream of prophets who had predicted that such an outcome would be inevitable if the people did not take seriously their vocation to incarnate the character of God for the sake of the world and start living God's way again.

In the eighth century BCE, Amos and Hosea spoke God's word to Israel, and Isaiah and Micah represented him to Judah. Their message was biting and disturbing. The nations were comfortable, economically prosperous, militarily secure, and religion was booming. There were worship centres everywhere. But the prophets came along and said that all this security was an illusion and that they were living on borrowed time. According to Amos 2:4–5, God indicts the people of Judah because in their apparent security and complacency they have abandoned God and begun to worship other gods. Things are going well without God, and they have set up idols of their own success and prosperity. But the whole sham edifice is going to crumble to bits before their very eyes. Their behaviour and apathy bear the seeds of their own destruction. But the people are too blind to see it.

In Amos 2:6–7, Israel is indicted for her institutionalised injustice, her toleration of oppression and perversion, and the fact that financial gain has become her god. Her worship is perverse. How can the people pretend to worship and honour God when they simultaneously grind into the dirt the heads of the poor and oppressed? God's people are supposed to be the image of their creator. When they behave like this, or tolerate behaviour like this, their words of faith are empty and vain. Privilege brings terrible responsibility (Amos 3:2), and these people are going to have to be faced with the real world. In their disaster, which they will perceive mistakenly as abandonment by their God, they will see their sham success and security for what they are. They will have the choice of interpreting their disaster either as innocent suffering and abandonment by a God who had conned them all along, or as a rude awakening to reality and a new opportunity to get things right again. Their choice will determine how soon they are restored.

Prior to the fall of Jerusalem to the Babylonians and the ensuing exile of 587 BCE, Jeremiah tried (albeit reluctantly) to alert the people to the gravity of their situation. They were taking God for granted and locating their security in religious institutions, buildings and rituals.[16] Their hypocrisy is blatant and they have learned nothing from the fate of Israel a century and a half ago. Exile is inevitable, even for the faithful and fraught Jeremiah himself.

The tragedy and desolation experienced by the exiled people of God cannot be overstated or exaggerated. Their misery and sense of despair were total. The book of Lamentations is a poetic lament which is both beautiful and heart-rending. Psalm 137 captures the poignancy of their predicament. How are the people to make sense of what has happened to them? God had promised them blessing, a land that would be the tangible evidence of his presence and favour, and a glorious future as the showpiece nation of the world. Have the people been deceived? Has God been defeated by the more powerful god of a pagan nation? How can they hope for a meaningful future when all they now experience is the apparent absence of God and abject disappointment? The book which best might help us understand this is Isaiah, so we will focus briefly on it.

HOPE FOR A CAPTIVE PEOPLE

In chapters 1 to 39 of Isaiah, we are introduced to the holiness of God, the corruption of his people and their institutions, and the inevitability of defeat and exile. God's judgement is to be perceived in military defeat and occupation, economic catastrophe, political destruction and the collapse of religious institutions. God is sickened by the propensity of the people to believe that as long as they are 'going to church' God will not notice the injustices and oppression they perpetrate and perpetuate. However, intertwined with this promise of punishment is the promise of eventual restoration, though God does what the people will find very difficult to do: he takes a long-term view of people, history and time.

In Douglas Adams' wonderful (and theologically fascinating) book, *The Hitchhiker's Guide to the Galaxy*,[17] there is a thing called the 'Total Perspective Vortex'. The idea is that when someone is nagging you or making life difficult for you, you put them in this TPV and they are shown how small and insignificant they are in the context of the whole universe. Chapters 40–55 of Isaiah are a bit like the TPV, but without the negative connotations. His message to his captive and disillusioned people is this: 'God has not finished with you yet! At the moment, you are blinded by your despair and disillusionment and you cannot understand my message. But your God is alive, despite his apparent absence from you for half a century. He does care about you and is about to return to you. Your history and your hard exile have not been without purpose. God is the Lord of history and he will prove it again soon. Be encouraged! God will meet you where you are, in your despair, with your justifiable fears, with your doubts about God, and your hope extinguished. And he will lift your spirits, build up your faith and re-establish your commitment.'

So, there is hope after all. But it is not a vague sort of wishful thinking. It does not deny the present suffering. It does not take the pain and the questions away. It does not demand instant solutions to complex situations. It does not make claims on God. Rather, it waits for God, endures the suffering and sees God's hand in it, working out his long-term purposes. This is the hope of believers throughout the centuries and in all parts of the world who know themselves to be just a part of God's wider purpose in the world, and who are convinced that their deliverance will come. A song sung by Christians in apartheid South Africa proclaimed, with absolute confidence in the love and justice of God:

> Freedom is coming.
> Oh yes, I know.[18]

Another song from the same challenging era spells out the understanding that God has a better, and longer-term, perspective on our suffering than we do:

> It doesn't matter if you should jail us,
> We are free and kept alive by hope.
> Our struggle's hard
> But vict'ry will
> Restore our lands
> To our hands.[19]

The remaining chapters of Isaiah are written to the remnant who have returned to the land and are needing encouragement as they begin to build a new future based on the experience and understanding of the past. There is evidently a debate about how the faith is to be expressed in religious worship and ritual. Even the return from the apparent disaster of exile was not the end of the story. The future would not now simply be rosy, but the hope of a messianic figure who would fulfil the hopes of Israel and all peoples had now firmly taken root. Rather confusingly for the Jews, this messianic person was to be a suffering servant and not an all-conquering military king.[20] God was to establish a new covenant with his people which had nothing to do with land, buildings and institutions, but with the heart and mind of his people.[21]

THE COMING OF THE MESSIAH

People often say that they would believe in Jesus if he came back and stood before them. If they could see him with their own eyes, they would believe him and give up everything for him. The precedent for this sort of thinking is not very encouraging. Many Jews expected the coming of a conquering king who would scatter the Roman Empire, deliver Israel into its rightful freedom and independence, and vindicate their faith for ever. Unfortunately for them, God had other ideas. He came incognito, took on human flesh and walked among us as a servant who refused the tools of power. People awaiting the coming of the Messiah were so impressed they crucified him. And we have no reason to think that we would recognise or welcome him any better today.

Jesus was quite outrageous in his claims. He assumed the role of a teacher who could improve on Moses. He claimed to be the fulfilment of all Israel's hopes and aspirations. He saw himself as the one pointed to by the prophets, the one who would establish a new covenant between God and people. He told stories which left his hearers in little doubt that he knew himself to have a crucial role to play in history. He healed the sick and forgave sins – something only God himself can do. He claimed not to *know* the way to God, but to *be* the way to God. He dared to call God 'Father'. He lived a lifestyle which many today would write off as being irresponsible and naive. He mixed with the wrong sorts of people. He knew he would die and that his death would not be the end; rather, he was convinced that his death would be the means to an end. To complete the earlier quotation from Colossians 1:19–20:

> For God was pleased to have all his fullness dwell in him, and through him to reconcile to himself all things, whether things on earth or things in heaven, by making peace through his blood, shed on the cross.

When Jesus talked to his friends about his death, they were quite bewildered and confused.[22] What was he talking about? How could the Messiah possibly be executed? Jesus did not try to convince them of something they could not possibly understand at that point. He told them they would understand later, after it was all over. And that is what happened. He scandalised religious expectations by suffering and dying in apparent failure. But on the third day his borrowed tomb was empty, his body (but not his shroud) gone. He appeared to many people, even eating breakfast with them. Then he left them alone. And at Pentecost, much to the surprise of his confused and frightened disciples, his promised Holy Spirit came in power and transformed their lives. He made ordinary people live extraordinary lives. Out of weakness, suffering and death had come resurrection, new life and restored hope. Death was not final after all. The hope of Israel *is* fulfilled in Jesus, and the remainder of human history will see his kingdom gradually grow in the world. The day will come when he will bring our hope to fulfilment by ending our history. This is what he promised and prefigured by his incarnation and resurrection. History is going somewhere. He will return.

This, in fact, is what eventually gripped the imagination of the disciples who had been devastated by the execution of their friend and then terrified by his apparent reappearances. They gradually developed an understanding of God's activity in the world through Jesus of Nazareth and, in the power of his Spirit, took seriously their vocation to now demonstrate to the world the character of God as seen in Jesus. They understood hope to lie in what God had done in raising Jesus from death, and saw their role to be to help the world to be caught up in this great mystery.

THE RECOVERY OF HOPE

The purpose of this brief excursion through biblical history is to show how hope in God is a hope in history.

For individuals, generations or entire nations, there can be times of questioning God's faithfulness or reality. Does our oppression or suffering necessarily imply God's absence? Or God's judgement? Or are we to learn to take a broader and longer perspective of God's activity and purpose in the world? It seems imperative that we who bear his name and claim to follow him also see ourselves as participating in the movement towards fulfilment, the coming of his kingdom. Our participation might involve suffering and oppression and pain. These are not to be fled from, but rather to be endured faithfully. Paul wrote from prison to the Philippian Christians:[23]

> For it has been granted to you on behalf of Christ not only to believe on him, but also to suffer for him, since you are going through the same struggle you saw I had, and now hear that I still have.

In some way, the remainder of this book is an exploration of what this sort of hope can mean to us in the world in which we live. What does this history of hope have to say to a widowed mother who finds every day a struggle? Or the parents of a handicapped child who struggle to love and care and make their marriage survive the strain? Or the young man who discovers he is to suffer and die from a terminal illness and wonders why? Or the person whose own life is smooth and relatively painless, yet who cannot understand the suffering of others? Or the community which sees itself as victimised and oppressed and looks for the God of justice?

These questions are important. What should be clear from our brief sketch of biblical history is that the hope and fate of the individual are inextricably intertwined with the hope and fate of a wider community. Jeremiah was faithful to God and suffered appallingly for it. He was not spared exile and pain and uncertainty.[24] The analysis of modern Western culture presented in the previous chapter showed how faith, hope and belief have been privatised and individualised. We claim individual rights and easily lose sight of the corporate and communal. Communities become fragmented, isolated and atomised. Millions of people passively watch the same programme at the same time on millions of private televisions. People die in isolation because nobody ever talked to them or even knew they were there. If we are to understand and grasp a genuine hope, which in turn will motivate and grasp us, we must regain the sense of corporate hope and a corporate critique of our culture.

If we need modern prophets, they are to be like those of the Bible. These men were not lunatics and fanatics who thought they could magically and infallibly predict the future. They were people who saw their society through God's eyes, and with God's values, and clearly saw what would happen if the current situation persisted. They knew that God would not abandon them in the long term, but they knew also that it would take a long time for the people to abandon their old ways, recover their vocation (to be the people of God for the sake of the world, not for the sake of Israel's prosperity) and learn the lesson.

We need to abandon the clamour for instant gratification of our aspirations and desires, both individual and social. Most of our great cathedrals took hundreds of years to build. Those who designed them and began work on them knew they would never see the completed structure. All they had was the satisfaction of pursuing the vision and fulfilling their particular part of the task. When Capability Brown laid out his beautiful gardens, he knew he would never see them at their best. He planted for the future and took a long-term view.

Hope that is founded and will not be disappointed must be rooted in the real world of history and experience. And it is to this that we will turn in the next chapter.

HOPE IN THE REAL WORLD

Hope has to be real. It has to be rooted in the past, the present and the future. It must have faced the reality of the past, be able to embrace the present, and provide a framework for walking fearlessly into the future – whatever the future should bring. It has to take seriously the real world we inhabit, and not be consigned to the realm of the purely other-worldly (which would be mere escapism). Hope has to be rooted in a faith that does not need to run away from experience, but which, on the contrary, transforms experience and makes it meaningful.

It is imperative, therefore, that we recover a proper understanding and experience of Christian hope within the real world. If we do not, then Christianity has nothing to say and makes no appeal of any significance. The gospel becomes yet another alternative way to escape, an ideology designed to make life tolerable. Christian hope must be capable of being made real to all people and all cultures. If not, we Christians are to be pitied above all people; for we are desperately deluded.

John Bell and Graham Maule, of the Iona Community, have written a vast number of imaginative new songs for the Church. They take very seriously the need for church music to be rooted in the real experiences of ordinary people. For them, as for the psalmists in the Old Testament, the whole of life is to be reflected in our worship, not just the nice spiritual bits. One of their songs expresses the hunger for reality and hope which we have been describing thus far. It is called 'The Sorrow':[1]

1. Don't tell me of a faith that fears
   To face the world around;
   Don't dull my mind with easy thoughts
   Of grace without a ground.

Ch. I need to know that God is real,
   I need to know that Christ can feel
   The need to touch and love and heal
   The world including me.

2. Don't speak of piety and prayers
   Absolved from human need;
   Don't talk of spirit without flesh,
   Like harvest without seed.

3. Don't sate my soul with common sense
   Distilled from ages past,
   Inept for those who fear the world's
   About to breathe its last.

4. Don't set the cross before my eyes
   Unless you tell the truth
   Of how the Lord who finds the lost
   Was often found uncouth.

5. So let the Gospel come alive
   In actions plain to see,
   In imitation of the one
   Whose love extends to me.

If faith is seen as an escape from reality, then the hope which stems from it is mere illusion. Jesus did not preach a gospel of fantasy, designed to exempt believers from suffering in the present or future; rather, he embodied a gospel of hope in the real world of suffering and struggle. He, who faced crucifixion and abandonment, spoke irrepressibly about joy. But how are we to know whether he and his bold promises can be trusted?

INCARNATION: GOD WITH US

The key to our understanding of hope is the incarnation: God with us here on earth. If a Christian's ultimate hope is in the will of God being done perfectly in a new heaven and a new earth, it makes sense only when understood in the light of God's coming among us. 'In the beginning was the Word, and the Word was with God, and the Word was God', writes John in the prologue to his Gospel.[2] This mystery is continued and culminates in one of the most astonishing statements in the Bible: 'The Word became flesh and dwelt [literally 'camped'] among us. We have seen his glory, the glory of the one and only Son, who came from the Father, full of grace and truth' (John 1:14).

According to John, God himself declined to remain above the dilemmas and dirt of human experience. Rather, he came and lived for a while among us. He lived as a real human being, not a sanitised mock-up. He was not simply pretending to be like us, but took upon himself the limitations of our humanity and became like us in every respect. In his letter to the church at Philippi, Paul quotes a contemporary hymn which expresses poetically what Jesus did:[3]

> Christ Jesus, being in very nature God,
>   did not consider equality with God
>   something to be grasped,
> but made himself nothing,
>   taking the very nature of a servant,
>   being made in human likeness.
> And being found in appearance as a man,
>   he humbled himself
>   and became obedient to death –
>   even death on a cross!

The pagan gods and goddesses of ancient Greece and Rome used their power to play with human life. The scandal of

Christianity is that God himself strips himself of his power and glory, becomes like his creation, and, vulnerable to their fickle passions, allows them to kill him.

If I had been God, I might have come to earth, had a good look around, then returned to the security of heaven at the earliest opportunity. I would have been appalled at the mess and apparent hopelessness of the enterprise. God, however, is different. His love for and commitment to his people transcend my fickle sense of convenience and judgement. God rolled up his sleeves and climbed down into the pit. He came to where we are. And that is indeed a mystery.

One of the lasting criticisms of the generals in the First World War was their tendency to issue orders from the relative security of the rear, and to die in bed with their boots off.[4] Meanwhile, the recipients of their orders, millions of troops, died horrible deaths amid mud and poison gas on the front lines. We ought never to demand of others what we are unwilling to ask of ourselves. God entered our world as it was and committed himself to it – warts and all.

An army officer told me once of the time a member of the royal family was due to visit his establishment. Instructions were issued that a special toilet be constructed for his use. This amused some and angered others. Many people wondered why he had special facilities made, especially at such expense. After all, a toilet is a toilet and only has one function whether the user is royal or rotten. The temptation we all face is to put on the best face for people we esteem as important. So the VIP does not have to experience the real-life conditions which ordinary people have to face.

In Jesus, God did not pull rank and claim extra facilities. He was born a Jew in a Palestine which was a restless corner of the Roman Empire. He was part of, and embraced the privileges of, his native culture. He had to grow up, learn, question, discover. He had to grow into a clear understanding of his own identity and mission. He had real parents and, presumably, a real adolescence. He faced the first-century equivalents of asking to borrow the family car. He learned a trade and, therefore, had to involve himself in the nitty-gritty of profit and loss, pricing mechanisms, economic realities, and the ethical dilemmas presented by conflicting demands and priorities.

He lived with and confronted real people in all walks of life. He embraced lepers and openly wept with the bereaved family and friends of a much-loved friend. Just when most men were established in family and work, he left home, family and security to become an itinerant teacher and preacher. He chose a small group of friends to be with him, enjoyed their enthusiasm and endured their stupidity without ever despising them. He did not shun conflict with arrogant religious and political authorities. He encountered opposition, isolation, desertion, ridicule and violence. He faced being misunderstood, misrepresented and having his reputation rubbished. He faced injustice at his trial without complaining and confronted the prospect of torture and death with real fear and apprehension. He was executed at the cosmopolitan crossroads of a commercial route with a mock crown upon his head.

Jesus never hoodwinked his followers into expecting anything different for themselves. He made it absolutely clear that to follow him might mean enormous cost and suffering. To carry a cross daily might one day lead to the porter being nailed to it.

Jesus took on human flesh, lived among us, and suffered as we suffer. He faced disappointment and temptation, got tired and hungry, and died as we all die. We cannot point a finger at him and accuse him of arrogance, ignorance or cowardice. He has been here and cannot be deceived.

It would be easy to picture Jesus as a victim. But that would only be half the story. Jesus was not simply on the receiving end of all that life could throw at him. He stood in the midst of the world's mess and challenged it head on. There was no place for fatalism in the mind of Jesus. He challenged assumptions about lifestyle and the values we adopt. He challenged assumptions about God and his values. He lived a radically different life and espoused a new set of values. He loved fiercely and assumed the right to forgive people's sins. He introduced his kingdom by healing the sick on the one hand and refusing to save himself on the other. He offered, in the boldest terms possible, to turn life itself upside down, to give purpose and meaning and value to all people. He transcended cultural barriers and derided petty divisions. He promised the inevitability of Judgement and justice for all: individuals, societies, churches, authorities, nations, cultures. And all this was rooted in love and servanthood, not power. Jesus shared the weakness of our humanity, thus allowing the power of death to be challenged face to face. He left death writhing on the ground of an empty tomb, racked by the agony of its own death-throes.

THE TRUTH ABOUT OURSELVES

It is one thing to be drawn by Jesus' promise that if we come to him he will never send us away thirsty.[5] It is quite another thing to accept the implications of it. For when we approach Jesus, the light of the world, the real state of our hearts and minds is illuminated. It is as if our eyes are opened and we see ourselves as we truly are. When we are with Jesus, we cannot hide or pretend. He has been here and he knows what we are like. But truth can be very unpalatable.

The problem with truth, as with hope, is that it is both a rare commodity and a much-abused word. We become accustomed to politicians treating truth like plasticine, bending it to fit their own desired shape. We hear a representative of government admitting to having lied and perjured himself in an Australian court of law – only he described his behaviour as 'having been economical with the truth'.[6] Winston Churchill preferred to speak of 'terminological inexactitudes' rather than 'lies'. At times of conflict or disaster, accusations of blame are fired across a no-man's land of popular bewilderment and increasing cynicism. Propaganda offers us 'palatable truth' – that is, that account of events which can be made to sound credible, but which is deemed politically expedient by those powerful people who control information.

In the hands of some religious people, truth becomes a weapon with which to inflict embarrassment or humiliation on those who dare to disagree with them. 'Truth' is defined by them alone, and everyone else is judged by their adherence to this self-referential orthodoxy.

Most of us are guilty of murder. No, we have not shot, stabbed or poisoned someone. But we have used exaggeration for effect, selecting facts and presenting them in a way that casts doubts upon someone else's integrity whilst reinforcing our own. We gossip, spread rumours and spoil reputations. In such ways, we kill people slowly and deliberately, labouring under the illusion that people thereby think better of us. We use truth, abuse it, exploit it selectively – and ultimately we pervert and deny it.

The result of all this is that we become caught up in a web of deceit in which Jesus will play no part. He said that the truth would set us free,[7] but we easily construct prisons out of the raw materials of image and pride. It is not just others who suffer; we also suffer who are unable to recognise the truth about ourselves.

Someone once told me with some enthusiasm about how successful he had been in sharing his faith with a friend. His clear impression was that his friend had been deeply moved and was seriously considering becoming a Christian. The truth was somewhat different. This man's friend had already spoken to me about how she had been put off Christians by this sort of aggression and arrogance. She had been talked at and not listened to. She had concluded that if being a Christian made you like that, she wanted nothing to do with it.

For many of us, it is difficult to face the truth about ourselves: that we are made in God's image and loved, but have also marred that image a million times. It can even be offensive because it strikes at the heart of our very being. But if we do not face reality we cannot change; our Christianity thus becomes a game – and the Gospels show us that Jesus is not impressed with the games we play. Even if we disagree with his diagnosis of our condition, we are still faced with the gulf between him and ourselves. Napoleon Bonaparte recognised this when he said: 'If Socrates were to enter this room, we would stand up and do him honour. If Jesus Christ were to enter this room, we would fall down on our knees and worship him.' To recognise the glory of Jesus (which is the character of God in him) is to be confronted with our need for grace, forgiveness and the freedom to start again.

And how do we see the truth about ourselves, if we are so prone to self-delusion? Experience suggests that we catch glimpses of who we really are. Like Cain's city, surrounded by defensive walls, we assume our own integrity and imperviousness; and then the walls are breached by insight, tragedy or joy – and we have to decide whether to venture beyond the walls into the unknown world beyond, or simply reinforce the walls so that they don't get breached again. Not surprisingly, the Gospels give us many examples of how people encounter the truth about themselves and find in this revelation either the door to freedom or the opportunity to re-build the wall.

SIMON'S PARTY

It is interesting when reading the Gospels to note which people Jesus welcomes and embraces. He loves the company of the poor and obviously 'sinful', and clearly they feel comfortable with him. Jesus always welcomes those who know they are in need. They do not need to be convinced that they are rotten sinners; they are already painfully aware of the fact – a point reinforced regularly by the self-righteous religious leaders. And it is always the self-righteous religious, the proud and arrogant, the independent and bigoted, for whom Jesus reserves harsh words: you are like tarted-up tombs, all pretty and well-presented on the outside, but putrid, decaying, stinking on the inside where it really matters![8] An imaginative look at one particular example from the Gospels might help to illustrate this point more clearly.

In Luke 7:36–50, Jesus is invited to a party. It is probable that, when inviting him to his home, Simon the Pharisee had in mind Jesus' entertainment value. We can imagine Simon getting his friends together and looking forward to the evening's amusement with this young upstart teacher. Jesus is the talk of the town, the trendy person to invite to dinner parties, the one to include among your acquaintances. He would at least make an interesting diversion from the normal routine of party chit-chat. Simon and his friends would not force the issue, but they would wait and see how the evening developed.

Jesus is not stupid. He knows why he is there and has accepted the invitation anyway. He never avoids conflict or shuns potentially embarrassing situations. So he enjoys his meal and does not deliberately stir up controversy in any way.

Suddenly, the party is disrupted by the arrival of a well-known woman of ill-repute. There is a stunned silence as she weeps over Jesus' feet, dries them with her own hair, and pours expensive perfume over them. Here is high drama indeed. What will Jesus do or say? How will he respond to this embarrassing intrusion? What will the other guests think? Should Simon do the decent thing and have the woman thrown out? What is going to happen to resolve this awkward situation? The tension in Luke's account is acute.

The reactions of the different people are both fascinating and significant. The other guests recognise the woman. They know all about her; perhaps some of them have known her more intimately in a more professional capacity. Their curiosity is mixed with embarrassment and disgust. If Jesus is worth his salt, he will not tolerate associating with the scum of the earth. He ought to look down on her shame, chastise and humiliate her, send her packing. After all, this would make the others feel that everything is OK with the world.

Simon really is caught on the horns of a dilemma. As the host, he is responsible for the well-being and comfort of his guests. This intrusion is deeply embarrassing, and he is possibly aware of his friends' mischievous interest in his response. His image, status and pride are at stake here. If he has the woman thrown out, he will be vulnerable to Jesus' response ... which as yet is unknown. If he does nothing, he will look weak, powerless, humiliated. He must take the responsibility of a host and do something, but things have now got a little out of control. Whatever he does is risky. So, tortured by indecision, he does nothing. He simply mutters to himself, suggesting that if Jesus really is a prophet he would know what sort of a woman this is and reject her. In this way, he neatly shifts responsibility from himself onto Jesus. And who can blame him?

Jesus sees exactly what is going on and grasps the initiative. He does not shout at Simon or moralise patronisingly about his arrogance. On the contrary, he does what he often does: he tells a story.

> Once upon a time, there were two men in debt to the same moneylender. One owed him fifty pounds and the other five. And since they were unable to pay, he generously cancelled both of their debts.

Jesus then invites Simon to respond and commit himself in words:

> Now, which one of them do you suppose will love him more?

Simon condemns himself out of his own mouth:

> I suppose it will be the one who has been more generously treated.

Jesus has made Simon draw the necessary conclusion for himself. He has not preached at him or spelled it all out. He has told a simple story and involved his hearers in responding publicly to it. Simon cannot turn around and accuse Jesus of rudeness or arrogance: he has made the damning statement with his own mouth. And I suspect that the implications of his response are not lost on Simon. Jesus confirms the rightness of Simon's response. Then he turns to the woman, whilst continuing to address Simon. Simon is left high and dry, his embarrassment and discomfort acute. Jesus' conclusion can be paraphrased as follows:

> Simon, you are my host and I am your guest. Yet you have neglected even the basic rules of hospitality. You

have treated me as not worth bothering with. My comfort is nothing to you. You think you are better than me. To have washed my feet would have been demeaning for you. You think your religiosity and power are adequate. You think your self-importance and status put you above such simple acts of hospitality as welcoming me to your home and offering me a drink. Simon, you are blind. You, too, are weak, feeble, sinful; but you cannot see it! You are blind to the truth about yourself. You are blinded and deceived by things that ultimately do not matter. And you have no excuse.

This woman does not need to be constantly reminded of her sinful nature, her past misdeeds, her awful reputation. She knows. But she has not hidden and pretended she was all right really. She has faced her deep need and recognised in me the source of forgiveness, acceptance, hope and peace. She has not formalised or broadcast her faith. She has not signed any statements of sound doctrine. She has simply exercised what faith she has in deep and profoundly moving humility. Because she has recognised her need of forgiveness, she has received forgiveness. Because she is forgiven, she is a new person; she is clean and has the right to start again. And, because of this, she is free in a way you do not understand and have never experienced, Simon.

In this episode, Jesus strips away the veneer of self-righteousness, successful religion and self-delusion. He confronts people with the naked truth about themselves: they all need forgiveness. Only those who recognise themselves in the woman can receive it and enjoy the freedom it brings. It is a very costly act of faith to meet Jesus in the company of those who can, with much justification, point the moral finger at our hypocrisy. But it is a cost worth meeting. It is the way of truth, the way to freedom and peace. It is the way of Jesus, and it goes to the heart of who we are as well as how we are.

THE CHALLENGE TO OUR VALUES

The sight of a crucified Christ challenges our self-righteousness and self-sufficiency. It challenges our pride and compels us to acknowledge our nakedness before him. But the crucified One also challenges our values. On the cross, as during his temptations in the wilderness, he throws down the gauntlet to our view of the world and its workings. He, who by his word created the universe, suffers humiliation at the hands of his creation and tells his followers to expect the same.

It is surely significant that so early in Matthew's narrative Jesus takes his chosen disciples off and begins to teach them the difference between his kingdom and the world.[9] The Beatitudes are a scandal, an affront to received and natural wisdom. The values of God's kingdom are radically different from those we instinctively feel to be natural.

The story has often been told of a vicar who, frustrated with the complacency and self-satisfaction of his congregation, erected a banner above the entrance to his church. The banner proclaimed in bold lettering: *Only Sinners Allowed in Here.* His congregation refused to attend church whilst the banner remained. It is commonly perceived that the church is for those who are comfortable and respectable and good; for surely it is they whom God finds most acceptable. This is blasphemous nonsense. The tragedy of this misconception cannot be overstated. A look back to the story of Simon's party shows clearly how Jesus responds to such people.

According to Jesus himself, who is the head of the Church and calls the Church 'my body', it is those who know their spiritual need who are blessed by God. They do not need convincing of their genuine spiritual poverty. The kingdom belongs to those who are meek

55

and those who long to be pure (but perhaps fear to begin the process). Those who do not judge, but are merciful, recognising their own need for mercy, will receive God's reward. It is those who suffer because of their concern to live God's way against the moods and trends of the world, who enjoy the glory of God's own kingdom. The world's values, according to which it is the successful achievers who are given high status, are shown up as fraudulent. They lead only to delusion, greed, pride and conflict. God's way is totally different.

I remember visiting a large evangelical church in the south of England at a time when I was a curate in the north. Whilst there, I felt a great temptation to compare it with the church I was currently serving. But the criteria which leaped into my mind to enable me to make a comparison were perverse: *How big is the congregation? How does the size of the congregation compare with the actual electoral roll? Have they modernised the church interior? How much money do they take in each year, and what proportion of it do they give away? Is there a strong lay leadership element in the church? How many housegroups do they have meeting regularly? Is there a competent music group or choir? Is the church seen to be successful?* These questions simply reflect the pragmatic economic values of my culture: big is better, success is what matters, numbers count, money speaks, and so on. The Jesus who chose only twelve fallible men and died deserted by all of them would surely be asking markedly different questions.

Jesus wants to know whether the Christians love him. He will know whether they love him (or not) by watching how they behave towards each other and the world beyond. Their love will not be proven in word or song or 'worship', not just in efficient organisation and careful administration, and not even in powerful preaching or well-conducted liturgy. Rather, Jesus looks for action, costly love and sacrificial service. He looks for leadership that is humble and honest. He looks for integrity and openness to learn, a willingness to be changed and mature. He is impressed only if he sees Christians loving one another as he loved us. But this sort of love is not easy. For it is a realistic love which acknowledges the depths of one another's sin, is not surprised by it, but loves through it. Jesus proved his love for us by dying for us while we were yet sinners.[10] He did not wait until we had cleaned ourselves up a bit before making his gesture. This is the sort of love we are commanded to have for one another. There is no other criterion that matters. This is the way of the crucified and risen Servant Lord.

It might sound odd to claim this as the way of personal liberation, but it is. It is not a matter of grovelling in the dirt or working up a sense of 'how bad I am'. It is simply a matter of recognising that I mess things up a million times and God is not surprised. But if God can set me free to carry on despite all this stuff, then I am bound to reflect that character in my dealings with others. So, I am not to trap people in their well-earned reputations, but to liberate them to shape a different future. I am not to be surprised by the goodness or badness of others, but to live graciously as one who has received grace. In the Lord's Prayer, it is summarised as: 'Forgive us our sins as we forgive those who have sinned against us'.

HOPE INCARNATE

It is common to speak about 'having a hope' or 'having faith'. The truth of the matter is that when we see Jesus in action and face the truth about ourselves, we are *grasped by hope and drawn into faith*. Jesus spoke a great deal about people finding eternal life in him. He boldly claimed that if people were to eat him, the Bread of life, they would never hunger. If they drank of the water he gives, they would never ever thirst again.[11] He said he would give eternal life to those who trust him. And yet this was never just a 'pie-in-the-sky' dream designed to string them along behind him. Rather, it was a promise made amid brute realism: if you follow me you will suffer; if you follow me you will do so with a cross on your shoulders; if you carry a cross you might well end up like me – nailed to it.[12]

In Jesus we find truth and reality. He flies in the face of a culture which worships the god of self-fulfilment by asserting that in order to find life we must first lose it.[13] In order to live, we must first die. This is not very romantic. For many people it is, frankly, downright offensive. But, however we react, it is true. And it is this same Jesus who guarantees that hopes which are rooted in him will not be disappointed. As we noted in the previous chapter, God's people often felt disappointed by God when things turned rough for them. They lacked a long-term perspective for what God was actually doing in history. But, as resurrection demonstrates, it is God who has the final word in this world, not violence, death and destruction. Read the history.

In order to make our hope of resurrection life realisable, Jesus first had to suffer a cross. He incarnated hope by willingly, though fearfully, submitting himself to the horrors of torture, death and abandonment by his Father ('My God, my God, why have you forsaken me?'), knowing that only by such apparent hopelessness could he guarantee any hope of a meaningful future. By being raised from the dead on the third day, thus fulfilling his predictions and promises, he made sense of all the horror and suffering. His promise of suffering to those who follow him was transformed from a sociological probability into a realistic necessity consistent with his life and teaching.

To share in the life of Jesus, we have first to share in his death. To grasp the hope of Jesus, we must first be grasped by the vision of Jesus. We must understand that the beginning of hope is the acceptance of our hopelessness. Only then can we be grasped by and begin to share in the hope that was Jesus'. A hope that does not begin with our *need* is mere wishful thinking; and Jesus has shown that such illusions are unnecessary. He has come among us, lived as one of us, experienced temptation, bewilderment, fear and death. And he has demonstrated that if our hope is rooted in him, we will not be disappointed.

> Christ has died:
> Christ is risen:
> Christ will come again.
> Alleluia!

THE ROOTS OF HOPE

The *good news* of Jesus Christ can actually be extremely *bad news*. The gospel of Jesus is not about our human competence and achievement. It is not about human success or beautiful images. It has nothing to do with pride or pomposity. It is fundamentally about failure, weakness, incompetence and need. A Christianity that masquerades as an invitation to health, wealth and material satisfaction bears no relation to the Jesus whose name it bears. It is a sham and an idol. It is based on a lie. And it will eventually bear the fruit of its own destruction. It is no accident that the symbol of Christianity is a cross, a symbol of execution, vulnerability, humility and weakness. For Jesus overturned human expectations of power and glory and presented the world with a scandal: a suffering Christ whose glory is to be found in his servanthood.

In the opening chapter of this book, we examined very briefly some of the effects of the Enlightenment on Western values and attitudes. We saw that God was not so much pushed out of the picture as quietly ignored. He became irrelevant to a humanity that was becoming increasingly self-sufficient and proud. Consequently, as God has receded in our consciousness, so we have begun to worship ourselves and our own achievements. The technological revolution of the twentieth century almost seemed to make the great humanist dream come true. However, our ability to abuse technology, along with our inability to match technical ingenuity with critical morality, has removed us from our pedestal. We are not gods after all. We are merely mortal, despite our cleverness, and we cry out for meaning behind our madness. Our idolatry of technology, power and achievement has led us down a blind alley. The problem is, however, that to retrace our steps in order to discover freedom is very painful. It hurts our pride. But that is what Jesus is all about.

Many years ago, and before PCs were even considered possible, I was responsible for teaching someone in my place of work how to use a particular computer system. If the office was to run smoothly, it was imperative that everybody in it used the system efficiently. However, having previously worked on a very different mainframe system, a new member of the branch thought this meant that he had nothing to learn. Affronted by any suggestion that he would have to take the time to be taught, he made it clear that he was sure he knew it all. In the following few weeks, he managed to have all his work rejected, and this in turn led to other people's work being affected and frustration levels increasing. Only then did he admit his need to learn – by which time, however, he also had to unlearn a good deal. This made his learning all the more difficult.

This is a simple illustration of the offence of Jesus' good news. He begins by showing us our need. Our response is often to refuse to accept this as the real state of affairs. We like to think we are in control of ourselves and our destiny. We think we can make our lives meaningful by changing our immediate circumstances. We think we are adequate and entirely self-sufficient. In short, we make God in our own image, but forget that the image can crumble. Only when we see ourselves as mortal, messy and needy can we begin to respond to Jesus. Only then can we begin to understand his gospel to be *good* news and not *bad*. Like the alcoholic, whose healing cannot begin until he utters the words 'I am an alcoholic', our hunger for reality cannot begin to be satisfied until we admit our inability to save ourselves.

At the beginning of Jesus' ministry, he receives a very clear rejection from the people of his own home town, Nazareth.[1] When he stands up to read in the synagogue on the Sabbath, he is among those who know him. They have watched him grow up and seen the way he has lived. They have worked with him and they have played with him. They entertain no false illusions about his integrity. They are intrigued and mystified, perhaps even vexed, by Jesus' decision to leave his job, his home and his family responsibilities (he is the eldest son of a widow). They are waiting for an explanation, a justification. If Jesus was a fraud, these people would have seen through his empty words within seconds of his opening his mouth.

Jesus reads from Isaiah 61:

> The Spirit of the Lord is on me,
>   because he has anointed me
>   to preach good news to the poor.
> He has sent me to proclaim
>   freedom for the prisoners
>   and recovery of sight for the blind,
>   to release the oppressed,
>   to proclaim the year of the Lord's favour.[2]

After reading the passage, Jesus sits down to begin teaching his congregation. He boldly claims that 'today this scripture is fulfilled in your hearing'. The atmosphere in the synagogue is electric, the drama poised to unfold. His hearers are amazed by his teaching and eloquence. 'Isn't this Joseph's son?' they ask, at this point responding positively to him and his words. However, Jesus clearly has no sense of timing and does not know when to stop. Instead of leaving off and basking in their praise, he carries on. He confronts the stubbornness of his own people to receive the truth about God, despite their privileged history. By the time he has finished, they are dragging him out and attempting to throw him off a cliff. Why?

Jesus could have accrued immense popularity and power if he had only told half the truth. But he insisted on telling people the unmitigated truth about themselves. Their problem was that they did not want to hear the truth; they were happier living with illusion and pretence. What they did not want was for somebody to come along and blow the whistle on their game. The reason he adopts Isaiah's words is that he knows who can receive the truth of his message: it is those who do not have a false view of themselves. It is the *poor*, who know they are poor and know they can do little about it. They do not need to be convinced of their need. It is the *prisoners*, who do not need to be convinced of the reality and gravity of their predicament. They know they are in jail and they know they deserve to be. They have not got a leg to stand on, and they know it. It is the *blind*, who know they cannot see and do not need to be persuaded that they need guidance. They do not have to be told that they are blind. It is the *oppressed*, who are fully aware that they are at the bottom of the pile. They know they are suffering unjustly and know there is little that they can do about it. They are powerless.

These, then, are the people who can receive the good news of Jesus. For them it is just that: good news. They have already experienced the bad news in their poverty, captivity, blindness and oppression. Jesus promises release and a new start. But it is very bad news for those who oppress, make or keep people blind, take people captive, or maintain other people's poverty. Jesus promises justice, 'the year of the Lord's favour'. This message is a threat to their status and lifestyle.

It is also very bad news for those who are blind, poor, oppressed or in prison, but who refuse to acknowledge their state. For so long as they pretend not to be blind, they will not understand their need to see. They will continue to bump into things and knock things over. They will live in darkness and convince themselves that it is normal. The offer of sight will not appeal to them. Some people will sit in their prison cell and refuse to move, even if the door is unlocked and opened for them. The prison can be a comfortable place to stay. It can, for example, prevent the prisoner from having to take responsibility for himself. He is not required to make decisions and face their consequences. The really bad news is that such people cannot even begin to receive the good news. They must first have the liberating humility to acknowledge their poverty, blindness, oppression and captivity.

What, then, are the things that obscure our vision of the truth? Certainly our pride and the desire to avoid the truth about our frail mortality get in the way of truth. It is very difficult for us to admit to a respectable society (or church) that we are blind or poor. It takes courage and a great deal of reckless faith to face the reality of our condition. It is easier to carry on worshipping our idols, living in a world of pretence.

IDOLS OF OUR TIME

Steve Turner is a journalist and writer specialising in rock music criticism. His interest in discovering the religious roots of modern popular music led him to write the penetrating and revealing book, *Hungry for Heaven*.[3] In an article defending his book's central thesis, Turner states: 'As a Christian with an interest in popular culture, I don't start with the question "Are people religious today?" but with the question, "What are people religious about today?"'[4] The point he is making is that when we cease worshipping God, we do not cease worshipping. We simply find, albeit sometimes unconsciously, another object for our worship. When the 'other object' replaces God as the centre of our affections and values, we find ourselves in the realms of what might be termed idol-worship. The most powerful and pervasive idols of our contemporary culture are power, success and self-fulfilment. These are the legacies of an age in which humanity assumes the role of the Creator and believes the lies of the god of this world. The trouble with idols, however, is that they either fall – or they go out of fashion. As such, to make them objects of worship is both short-sighted and ridiculous.

Power: 'Money makes the world go around ...' proclaims the song from the musical *Cabaret*. But this is not true. It is power that makes the world go around, and money is just one aspect of power. Power essentially has to do with relationships and values. The German philosopher responsible for the premature announcement of God's demise, Friedrich Nietzsche, said: 'Wherever I found a living creature, I found the unconditioned will to power, to overpower'.[5] It is entirely possible for power to be exercised for the benefit of all. But it can also be, and very often is, abused and misused, whether it be the desire to establish an ideological dogma in society or the ability to manipulate one's husband or wife in order to get one's own way. Of course, we are usually totally unaware that we are playing a power game. But, where there are two people in a relationship of any sort, the situation is a political one, and power is the name of the game. Countries exercise military, economic, ideological and political power over other countries. The fact that one group or person possesses power implies that the other group or person does not.

This is not the place to perform a critical analysis of power in all its forms. It will suffice our purposes to state that power is intoxicating and that it feeds on success.

This is true of all relationships and is particularly true in religious establishments. The power of the priest might have been diminished under the onslaught of secular thinking, but that does not mean that religious authorities have lost their power. The threat of eternal damnation can still be perversely held over people in order to keep them in line (or in church). The threat of God's displeasure can still be used unwittingly to make people feel guilty for not having performed their devotional duty today. We can make God in any image to suit the purpose of our maintaining the status quo: holding on to power.

It is important to acknowledge the reality of power games within religious societies before going on to criticise the secular idols of success. Christians cannot point the finger at the oh-so-wicked-world as if we are pure and untainted by such evils. But neither is it my intention to point the finger at the Church (as many do). In humility we are to face up to reality, confront the truth about our weakness and fallenness, and learn to recognise our failures. Only then can we begin to change. And we are all in the same boat.

That said, power is very much the god of our age. We worship our technological achievements, the power and seductive quality of our cars. In our advertising, we play upon people's greed, love of glamour, sexual weakness, self-image. We say that owning a Porsche makes you more valuable and powerful than a man who owns a bike. To be a corporate executive in a multinational company with millions of dollars at your disposal makes you more successful and powerful (and, therefore, more valuable) than the woman who looks after her children and struggles to make ends meet. The fact that the executive might be playing a high-risk game, using millions of other people's livelihoods as pawns, only adds to the mystique. A pop singer, or actor, who lives up to an image and has an industry built up around her, can earn fame and fortune virtually overnight. She becomes an object for money-making. She is valued for how much money she can generate. Her world might become empty and sad, her image gradually devouring her own inherent self-value. But that is fine so long as she remains a star. When she loses her figure or her voice, she can be replaced by the next *new* thing. Novelty can be very powerful.

Success: Those who are successful are worth more than those who are ordinary or those who just fail. We worship the entrepreneur and the achiever. We admire the strength of those who get to the top, whatever the cost of getting there and whoever got trampled on along the way. The single-minded selfishness that drives a man to prove himself better than others is rewarded by social status and material reward. And when the rich and successful instigate public mutual-admiration ceremonies (at which they all congratulate each other for being so rich and successful), we watch them on our television screens and share in their reflected glory. We are easily seduced by the gods of success and self-sufficiency.

Once again, Christians are not exempt from worshipping these idols. We judge the success of evangelists by numbers attending meetings, numbers 'going forward', numbers taking literature or 'praying the prayer'. (John 6 is a bit of an embarrassment in this respect: Jesus begins with 5000 people and, after preaching, loses the lot.) Yet these people are made of flesh and blood. They can get cancer, have headaches and suffer from haemorrhoids. Advertising for big Christian events (concerts, conferences, etc.) plays on the attractive quality of the big names. These Christian preachers and teachers are so successful that they can guarantee 'Spirit-led worship', 'powerful Spirit-inspired Bible teaching', 'a powerful experience of God's healing'. Am I missing something here, or are we being seduced by the 'god of this world'? Do we simply satisfy our personal or corporate craving for success and power by adhering to such 'successful' people? Those responsible for much of the advertising for big Christian events ought to examine the motivation and values behind their image-presentation. I suspect that this could be a very painful exercise.

Self-fulfilment: I am the centre of the universe. Only I matter. If my self-fulfilment (whatever that means) is being hampered by the demands of other people, I am quite within my moral rights to free myself from them. The pursuit of my personal happiness is the greatest good, and I am justified in doing anything which will promote it. If other people get hurt, that is their fault for not being as strong and successful as I am in the business of living. This individualism lies at the heart of contemporary thinking and values, and it is a false god, an idol, a sham which will disappoint and frustrate those who worship it.

Christians must first ask whether they also worship this idol. There is increasing talk about self-fulfilment in the (so-called) 'ministry'. The greatest good for some people is that they are 'fulfilled' in their job or role. There is nothing wrong with feeling fulfilled, contented or useful, but these must not become the standards by which we measure what is valuable or important. I wonder if Jesus felt fulfilled in the Garden of Gethsemane. The costly demands of love and service will inevitably clash violently with the attraction of self-fulfilment from time to time. The conflict cannot be avoided. But it is easily ignored.

THE GOOD NEWS

The good news is that these gods are made of straw, albeit very strong, flexible and durable straw. Jesus thought of such idols as dross. He shocked his contemporaries by contradicting these ephemeral values. Life is to be found

[handwritten annotation at top: Power, Success, Self fulfillment - "Gods of our time/age" → riddled with holes → they promise much but delivers nothing]

in death. The only success that matters in God's eyes is faithfulness to him and humble, self-sacrificial service of other people (especially our enemies).[6] For God, ultimate power is revealed in a crumpled corpse hanging from a rough-hewn gallows. The only way to fulfil ourselves is by first denying ourselves. This message was a scandal in the first century, and it would appear that its reception has not changed significantly since then.

The good news is that these gods have fallen. We need not worship them any longer. They have been emptied of their substance and power. They have been displayed before the world by a crucified God and shown to be riddled with holes. They promised much and delivered nothing. The good news is that we need not sell our souls for a transient illusion of glory. Instead, we can share in the real, substantial and costly glory of God himself. We can be released from the cultural prison which values us according to our achievement, success, power and image. We can begin to live differently.

We do this by acknowledging our weakness and failure. We allow ourselves to be stripped of the veneers of respectability and self-sufficiency which keep our public image intact. We see the open prison door and walk out through it. We confront the illusions about ourselves which we hold dear. We admit our 'lostness'. And we see our essential value lying in the fact that God values us for who we are, not for what we achieve. For he sees to the heart of our reality and he loves us anyway.

THE GRACE OF GOD[7]

If you are sitting in a prison cell, enduring the punishment you deserve, you cannot simply open the door and walk out into freedom. However, if the door was opened from the outside by someone else, you would then have to choose whether or not to get up and leave your captivity behind you. As we remarked earlier, it is quite possible to have the cell door unlocked and opened and yet to remain inside, unwilling or afraid to leave the security of those four walls. The important feature to notice here, though, is that the door has to be opened from the outside. The prisoner cannot let himself out. He cannot set himself free. He requires an outside agent who will set him free.

It is no accident or coincidence, therefore, that Jesus took the words of Isaiah upon himself. The poor are often powerless to change their circumstances; they cannot become rich overnight just by deciding to become so. They might need outside support and encouragement. The inarticulate, those who, because of their powerlessness and poverty, lack a voice, need others to speak on their behalf in order that their words might be heard. Likewise, the oppressed are often unable to achieve their own liberation while their suffering continues at the hands of those who are powerful. The blind man cannot remove his own cataracts or re-attach his own retina; he requires a skilled surgeon to intervene and do the job for him. The prisoner has to be released by an outside agent. That is what God does for those who know their need and bury their illusions.

The heart of the good news of Jesus Christ is that we cannot save ourselves. Instead, as in Israel's seminal experience in the Exodus, God himself brings about our liberation. God himself has unlocked the door of our prison and beckons us to come out into the light of day. He calls us to leave behind our captivity to image, ego or success and invites us to step into the freedom and risk of life outside the cell. And the response we make is left up to us. He will not force us out into the fresh air if we do not want to go.

It is both humbling and offensive to us that we need an outside agent to set us free. We are used to the idea that *we* control our own lives and destinies. We are clever and sophisticated. Any idea of faith in someone greater than our power to imagine is merely a crutch for the weak and afflicted. So the cross of Christ, his unique claim to be the way to the Father, his offer of freedom appears to be an offence. It hurts our pride and scandalises our sense of dignity. It cannot be so simple, it cannot be true. After all, nothing is free in this world, is it?

But the grace of God is like a gift, and the thing about a gift is that the recipient has no right to it. He cannot lay any claim to it or demand it. It is purely and simply the prerogative of the giver to choose the gift and the recipient. All the recipient can do is to hold out a hand and receive it. It is not coincidental that the memorial meal Jesus bequeathed us has us holding out empty hands to receive bread and wine.

Once, I was doing a children's talk in a church in the south-west of England. I had a packet of sweets wrapped in birthday paper. By way of illustration, I had a child come out to the front of the church, and we talked about the gift I had in my hands. At first, the child was sure he wanted to receive the gift, though he had no idea what was in it. By the time we had finished discussing what might be in it, he was less sure he wanted to take the risk. In the end, I could not get him to take the parcel from me. The boy could only receive the gift if I offered it to him and was not in a position to demand it. But I could not force him to receive it. However hard I might press him to take it, it is ultimately his choice. God offers us freedom from slavery to our idols. Whether we accept this liberation to a new life is very much down to us. Our response is crucial.

GRACE IMPLIES FORGIVENESS

All this would be fine if we just left it there. God offers us freedom and a new life. But the gift of God's grace is forgiveness as the licence to start afresh. Forgiveness presupposes guilt, and guilt is regarded by modern, psychologically sophisticated people as unnecessary and unhelpful: after all, a morality that is merely relative and arbitrary must mean that any attitude or behaviour can be justified in some way. But Jesus saw that guilt was not just an unhealthy feeling of self-denigration; rather, guilt is the state we are in. If I have committed a crime, it does not matter whether I *feel* guilty or not. I might be deluded and believe someone else did it. But none of that can change the fact that I did it. I am guilty of the crime. Even if the jury acquits me in court, it does not change my status as the guilty party.

The basic understanding of human nature in the Bible is that everyone is guilty of worshipping idols and compromising the vocation given to us as beings who are made in the image of God – whether they acknowledge the fact or not. That guilt can be ignored or it can be faced squarely and honestly. Only when it is acknowledged can there be forgiveness. Therefore, forgiveness cannot be earned or claimed as of right. It cannot be demanded or assumed. It can only be received with thanks and humility.

Now, far from being bad news, this encounter with our need can be the most liberating event in our lives. Charles Wesley described his own experience in his famous hymn based on Romans 5:8:

> Long my imprisoned spirit lay
> Fast bound in sin and nature's night;
> Thine eye diffused a quickening ray, –

> I woke, the dungeon flamed with light;
> My chains fell off, my heart was free,
> I rose, went forth and followed Thee.[8]

When we receive God's gift of forgiveness and a new start in life, we sound the death-knell of pride and arrogance. The greatest thing in the world has happened, and yet we did nothing to achieve it. Hence, there can be no place for pride. As the apostle Paul wrote to the church in Ephesus:

> For it is by grace you have been saved, through faith – and this not from yourselves, it is the gift of God – not by works, so that no one can boast?[9]

❋ THE HUMILITY OF HOPE ❋

The liberation we have just described not only frees us from self-condemnation and pride; it also sets us free from the need to judge others. If I am healed by God's grace alone, then I have neither the right nor the liberty self-righteously to point the finger of guilt or accusation at anybody else. The fruit of this liberation is to make me more like Jesus. And that means that I will now live as a servant, not a master. It means I will now carry a cross, not stones to throw at other people (however much they might deserve it). It means I will now embrace suffering or deprivation for Christ's sake, and not worship at the shrines of success and power. This is the way of Jesus. And it is the way of those who bear his name, too.

The New Testament letters address the call of Jesus to his friends (just prior to his death) to love one another as Christ has loved them. For example, the Philippian Christians are told to abandon their class divisions whereby Roman citizens in the Church have higher status than the others (Philippians 2:1–11). The basis of Paul's call to Christians to love and serve one another lies simply in the acknowledgement that none of us has any right to stand in judgement on anyone else because we all know ourselves to be forgiven sinners who have received grace as a gift. It is as simple as that.

This leaves open the possibility of transformation. Experiencing the forgiveness of God through Jesus does not make us into perfect saints. It makes us into free, but ragged, saints. And life becomes a process of being transformed by God into his image. This, once again, is utterly liberating. The knowledge that God has set me free and let me loose in his world to love and serve him means that I need not be afraid of being honest about failure and reality. God is transforming me, but he has not finished yet. I must be patient, and others must be patient with me. If I am to live honestly, open to transformation and change, I am inevitably going to make mistakes. Other people (particularly other Christians) are going to despair of me at times, even failing to recognise Jesus in me. But even that cannot prevent God from leading me into light. For God is the one who forgives and restores, who empowers me to walk his way and live with the untidiness of it all.

Hope lies in the possibility of transformation. It is rooted in the humility which stems from an honest acknowledgement of need and acceptance of forgiveness. It sets the believer free to make mistakes and run risks, secure in the knowledge that God takes a much longer-term view of things than we often do. It strips the Christian of the need for pretence and image-construction. It is the most wonderful and renewing experience on earth.

JESUS AND A NAUGHTY LADY

One of the most powerful and dramatic stories in the New Testament is recorded in John 8. Jesus has gone to the temple and has sat down to teach the people who want to listen to him. He has not been talking for long when there is a disturbance and his flow is interrupted. The religious authorities and teachers appear, dragging with them a woman who has been caught in the act of adultery. They humiliate her and make her stand in full public gaze while they try to catch Jesus out. This woman is a pawn in their game, an object to be used for their own (theological) ends. She can be humiliated by those seeking religious self-justification. Her predicament is an awful one.

Before continuing with the story, it is worth asking a few pertinent questions. How did these people know where to find her? Had they visited her previously? Was she well known for her loose living? How had they managed to catch her 'in the act of adultery'? Had they set her up? How did they know when to interrupt her act of adultery? Who was the man involved? Where was he now? What responsibility did he take? Why did the religious teachers humiliate the woman and, by implication, exonerate the man? It would be very interesting to know the answers to these questions.

Anyway, the drama is intense. They confront Jesus with this woman and quote Scripture to him. The law of Moses commands such a woman to be stoned. If Jesus is a good Jew, he must agree with the law of Moses. This would mean contradicting his teaching thus far and participating in the condemnation of the woman. However, if he does not go along with the prescriptions of the Mosaic law, he is implicitly claiming the right to reinterpret the law. To do so would be to claim to be greater than Moses; in fact it would be to assume the mantle of God. To do this would be to lay himself open to a charge of blasphemy. These teachers must have spent ages working on this one; they really think they have caught Jesus in their trap.

Jesus does not respond immediately. With a wonderful sense of timing, he bends down and starts to write in the dust with his finger. People strain forward to see what he is writing. The tension is high, the suspense is terrible. The woman stands there humiliated and afraid, facing a possible death sentence. Everyone is hanging on Jesus' response. But Jesus does not respond. He just keeps on writing in the dust.

What was he writing? No one knows, though many have speculated. Was he just doodling whilst trying to think his way out of this mess? Or was he deliberately trying to raise the sense of expectation and heighten the drama? Was he trying to make the crowd and his inquisitors feel uneasy and exposed? We cannot know what was going on in Jesus' mind or what he was writing on the ground. But we can imagine that the suspense was killing the onlookers. Trying to bait Jesus must have been an infuriating exercise: the inquisitors burst in, adrenalin flowing, savouring the juices of imminent victory over this awkward and embarrassing upstart ... and Jesus bursts their bubble by making them wait.

In their exasperation and excitement, they press Jesus to reply. Perhaps they sense that they have got him in a corner. They want to hear him condemn himself out of his own mouth. Jesus eventually chooses to straighten himself up and look them in the eye. 'If any one of you is without sin, let him be the first to throw a stone at her.' Then he stoops down again and carries on writing in the dust. There is a silence. Everybody looks at the ground. Thoughts race around confused minds. Jesus, in one sentence, has turned the tables completely around. He has removed the onus of response and moral responsibility from himself and planted it firmly where it belongs. Jesus has not condemned his inquisitors or harangued them for their treatment of the woman. He has not preached a sermon at them, designed to convince them of their own sinfulness. He has simply made a statement, inviting them to address their own holiness before condemning the unholiness of someone else.

The interesting thing about this narrative is the inclusion of a detail which at first sight appears insignificant. 'At this, those who heard began to go away one at a time, *the older ones first*, until only Jesus was left, with the woman still standing there' (verse 9). Why did the older ones leave the scene first? Perhaps it is because they had lived longer, had made great moral resolutions in the past only to see them crumble, and knew the reality of sin and weakness. It is often younger people who most fiercely judge the wrongs and shortcomings of others. It is often younger people who pursue self-righteous campaigns, who are impatient with the failures of others. Age and experience can bring wisdom, a willingness to forgive, and a greater humility – or just a weariness with the constant pressure to condemn other people for 'not being like us'.

The point is that nobody had the right to point an accusatory finger at this woman. When they were confronted with their own failure and weakness, their own inability to save themselves, they knew they had no right to condemn anybody else. We can only guess imaginatively at what the woman was feeling at this point. A few moments ago she was humiliated and pursued; now she is free and alone with this enigmatic man. He has not accused her or abused her. He, who had power to exercise over her, has declined to do so. He, who had the moral right to condemn and upbraid her, looks her in the eye and treats her with dignity. He does not give her a stiff talking to, nor does he tell her to grovel for forgiveness. On the contrary, he actually asks what appears to be a silly question: 'Woman, where are they? Has no one condemned you?' In asking this question, he invites her to say it with her own mouth:

'No one, sir', she said. She cannot believe her ears. After all the humiliation and fear, her encounter with Jesus has freed her from the condemnation of her accusers.

In a supreme response of love and grace, Jesus sends the woman on her way. 'Then neither do I condemn you,' Jesus declared. 'Go now and leave your life of sin.' She knows she does not deserve this. She has been faced with the truth about herself and her sin. And so have all those who, self-righteously, tried to accuse her of being worse than themselves. Jesus set her free and sent the accusers away to ponder their own need.

This is a very powerful story of God's grace. It has clear implications for our relationships with one another. When we find ourselves sneering at the guilt or sin of others, we ought to remember Jesus and the woman. When we see other Christians sinning wildly, we must respond in humility, not judgement.

Several years ago, I was delighted to hear of the disgrace of the television evangelists in America. The sight of a man who had extracted millions of dollars from ordinary people in the name of Christ, abusing power and responsibility, weeping with shame in a courtroom made me laugh. My thoughts were that this man had got what he deserved, and I found myself hoping that his misery would be total. When I examined my reaction to this, I was both ashamed and horrified. My reaction betrayed the fact that I thought I was better than he, that I somehow deserved God's favour more than he did. God was on my side. I should have been on my knees, weeping with compassion for a man made in the image of God and for whom Jesus had died. Yes, he deserved justice and his prison sentence. But in God's eyes he is as deserving of grace as I am. If we are saved, we are saved by God's grace alone. I have nothing at all to boast about.[10]

TWO OBSERVATIONS

The Christian community is to be one of love and forgiveness, not judgement and status. If we walk the way of Jesus, we must love as he loved us. This means loving the unlovely and the unlovable. This means taking seriously the Lord's Prayer, according to which God's forgiveness of us is contingent upon our forgiving those who offend us. It means a community strong on justice, strong on love, rooted in forgiveness and humility. It means a community in which the sting of past failure is drawn and not held up as evidence any time someone we dislike or distrust puts a foot wrong.

Christians, rooted in humility, must allow one another the freedom to admit weakness and doubt. Too many Christians, claiming to have been set free by Jesus, are in chains to their sense of shame. It is not that Jesus is afraid of their weakness; rather, it is that other Christians can be self-righteous and judgemental. It is the expectation that if we are honest about our failure, fears, doubts or questions, we will lose spiritual status in the eyes of those we call our brothers and sisters. But perfect love casts out fear, and many Christians need to be set free from the prisons erected by other Christians. God is not fooled; he knows our hearts and minds. And he is clearly not as shocked by what he sees as we are. Jesus came because he *knew* what we are like. We need to learn to love one another as he loves us.

THE ROOTS OF HOPE

We have observed that the roots of hope are to be found embedded in the humble acceptance of the need for and possibility of transformation. This possibility is itself rooted in the grace of God. The experience of God's grace in forgiveness necessitates a whole new way of living and seeing other people. A new community is born. There is a temptation, however, for the good news of Jesus to be made more palatable, for the offensiveness to be removed. Jesus refused to make his gospel more palatable. In a world where weakness was a dirty word, he declined to make his message more macho. Rather, he was happy to let the gospel be merely offensive. He resisted the pressure to waive the rules a little in order to squeeze more (influential) people into his kingdom.

A rich young man comes to Jesus, genuinely searching for hope and meaning and claiming to be living a very holy life. Jesus does not despise his claims. According to Mark's Gospel, Jesus 'looked at him and loved him'.[11] Jesus suggests that he sell all his possessions and give the proceeds to the poor. Jesus has struck the nail on the head. For this is the young man's real security, his real god. But he cannot face the cost and goes away sad. Many evangelists would have run after him, saying that he could pay it in instalments if he wished. Jesus does not pursue him. The man has made his choice. He is not hungry enough for hope.

I always thought that it would have been a sign of great *strength* for the man to give up his wealth and follow Jesus. Surely this could not be described as a gospel of *weakness*. This is true. But if the young man had made himself poor, as Jesus seems to be suggesting, he would then have experienced something new: vulnerability, weakness, insecurity, need, dependence. Perhaps even fear. The roots of hope are to be found here.

6

THE KINGDOM OF HOPE

I sometimes wonder if the first friends of Jesus ever really understood just how seditious he actually was. They had seen him in conflict with the religious authorities. They had heard him say some outrageous things about himself and the crisis he forced upon those who encountered him. But even when they asked him how to pray, he did not simply emit platitudes and clichés. He went straight to the heart of those who wished to learn and unambiguously indicated the personal costliness and commitment of prayer and piety. He said: 'Your kingdom come, your will be done on earth as it is in heaven' (Matthew 6:10).

The prayer from which this sentence is taken has been called the most beautiful prayer ever conceived. And therein lies the problem. Beauty can be a terrible thing because it encourages the beholder to stand back and to admire from a distance. The subject becomes an object, and its power is lost. In this case, the prayer remains 'the Lord's Prayer' and does not become 'our' or 'my' prayer.

I was trained professionally as a linguist. Indeed, I spent four years working as a linguist specialist within British government service. Working with words can be an exhilarating, yet frightening, experience. Words are a beautiful, complex and powerful tool for communication and, therefore, need to be respected, not wasted. In the Church, there are those who wish to retain ancient words and phrases in Christian worship, seeing in their familiarity and beauty a way to approach God. But there are also those who wish to modernise all religious and liturgical language in order to make it 'intelligible' to a contemporary world which is, in many respects, post-Christian. I sympathise with both. Of course, it should be obvious that broad intelligibility and linguistic beauty are not incompatible. The point to note here, however, is that the love of beauty in the form of linguistic expression can eventually obscure the crude power of the message which the language is intended to convey. It is possible for us to know the words, love the phrases, enjoy the sentiments, bathe in the associations and miss the point they are making. (For example, listen to some beautiful settings of 'The Magnificat' and then read the deep subversiveness of the text itself.)

I remember many years ago leading a study of the Lord's Prayer with a group of teenagers, most of whom had grown up in the Church and had Christian families. The object of our study met with some reluctance initi-ally, for teenagers often find rehearsal of the familiar to be boring. I suggested that this prayer is more, much more, than an empty and anodyne assembly of nice religious thoughts, and confidently asserted that the content of the prayer is actually quite revolutionary. This statement met with a blank silence. At the end of the study, one eighteen-year-old said, 'I never knew that this is what the prayer is all about'. I replied that it is not an easy prayer to pray because the implications for my own life, motivation and commitment are so utterly radical. She was silent for a moment, then said again, 'I never realised'. This dawning realisation was a cause of hope, for her eyes had been opened to see beyond the familiarity of the words and glimpse the power and demands of them. Life can never be the same again. Never again can that prayer be merely a simple and vain repetition of pious aspiration.

The 'truth' which that girl perceived for the first time was very simple. It is easy to call God 'our Father' and to praise him. It is much more awesome to pray that his kingdom might come. Why? Because the coming of the kingdom means that God's will, done perfectly and consistently in heaven, is to be done here on earth. When I pray that prayer, asking God to bring in his kingdom in the world I inhabit, I am inviting God to begin with me. I am committing myself to conforming to God's will, his way of seeing the world, his way of living and loving. And that is both revolutionary and extremely costly. It is conversion. It is also the invitation to enjoy what Jesus calls 'abundant life', life in all its fullness (John 10:10).

JESUS AND THE KINGDOM

In the previous chapter, we saw how the reality of hope lies in the possibility of being changed. It begins with the unambiguous acknowledgement of our need to change and be changed by God. It is a hope that is rooted in humble acceptance of God's grace. It is worked out in self-denying and loving service of those for whom Jesus also lived and died. The life lived thus is part of what it means to be in the kingdom of God.

The concept of the kingdom of God is a thoroughly dynamic one. The kingdom is not a destination to be arrived at, nor is it merely a place to inhabit. It is not just a good idea. When Jesus begins his preaching ministry, his essential message is concise and absolutely clear: 'Repent, for the kingdom of God is near'.[1] We are called to repent *in response* to the approach or presence of the kingdom. Jesus entertained no illusions that people could encounter the kingdom of God and remain unchanged. The kingdom provokes a crisis and demands a clear response.

Why? Because the 'kingdom' could be translated as 'the presence' of God; and where God is present we become powerfully conscious of our 'being loved' and of our need of grace. 'Repentance' means literally 'to change our mind' – to change the way we look, see, think and live in order to see through God's eyes. It involves a process of allowing our mindset to be re-shaped as we learn to think differently. It is easy to present a gospel which simply comforts and satisfies. A gospel which meets needs will always be welcome, but Jesus preaches a gospel which must be acted upon. To encounter God is to see ourselves for who we really are; it is to see and acknowledge the truth about ourselves. Repentance is not just words. Neither is it simply the *willingness* to make minor adaptations sometime in the future, a grudging nod in the direction of God. It is radical in the fullest sense of the word: it penetrates to the roots of our being, our values and our behaviour. It is revolutionary, or it is not repentance.

If I am standing on a railway line and hear the rumbling of an approaching train, I have to make a choice: I can move off the tracks to the right or to the left, or I can stay where I am and get squashed by the inevitable encounter with the engine. It is not enough for me to decide that the wisest move would be to step away from the tracks in one direction or the other. My intellectual agreement that this would be the best and most appropriate action, accompanied by its great emotional power and compulsion, will not prevent my being hit by the train. I must make a choice and act upon it. I might not be sure what lies on either side of the tracks, but that ignorance cannot be allowed to stop me moving.

The kingdom of God comes with compelling and devastating power. I must decide whether to commit myself (all that I am and have) to it. Having decided, I must act accordingly. To claim allegiance to the kingdom of God, and yet to remain unchanged by it, is to live a lie, to suffer a grave delusion. We are to seek first the kingdom (Matthew 6:33). In the words of Jim Wallis, leader of the Sojourners Community in Washington D.C., 'to be Christian is to be possessed and dominated by the kingdom of God'.[2] Jesus inaugurates his kingdom, a whole new order in human affairs. He establishes a new kind of community, empowered by the Spirit of God himself to demonstrate God's new creation, his values. Ordinary people are called to leave their old allegiances and to live new lives in conspicuous contradiction to the values and standards of the old world. When we enter God's kingdom, we do so in response to his grace and because the kingdom itself is upon us.

We noted early in Chapter 2 that to be locked in the past, without hope of transformation, is to be truly hopeless. The most marvellous feature of the coming of the kingdom of God is the fact that it demands and promises transformation. People who met Jesus were forced into a crisis: what are they to do with him? What judgement are they to make about him? How are they going to respond to him? Those who were locked into the past or present, or were constrained by fears about the future, found him offensive and disturbing. Their antipathy to him and his challenge led them to crucify him. Those who were prepared to trust him and his sort of kingdom found their lives turned upside down and inside out. For many of Jesus' early followers, their experience of release from the prison of their past life and reputation was so powerful and renewing that it prepared them for terrible suffering and eventual execution.

The kingdom Jesus owns is one which demands full allegiance. However, most of us know we cannot live like Jesus. Many people fail to enter the kingdom because they fear that they cannot live up to the standards God sets. For some, there is no point in even beginning because failure is as certain as day follows night. But this is a false and unnecessary fear. The basic credential for entering the kingdom is, as we have stressed repeatedly throughout this book, acknowledgement of our need, the abandonment of our illusions. We receive forgiveness and the freedom to start again. We are a new creation in Christ; the old life, along with all its patterns and values, has died. We have a new identity, a new allegiance, a new hope. And thus can we have real peace with God and ourselves. We are set free to be open and honest. The need to preserve an image, to pretend or hide, has gone. We have been set free to live a new life, empowered to accept gradual transformation, and to learn to discern and follow in the way of God's will.

THE NATURE OF THE KINGDOM

The kingdom is where the king lives. No king, no kingdom. There are many political kingdoms in the world in which the king (or queen) has no real power or authority. The monarch's role is constitutionally prescribed and in many ways nominal. He or she cannot do much to effect change or to shape the values and lifestyle of the people. This is not a notion shared by Jesus' understanding of God's kingdom. The kingdom is where the king is. He rules according to certain precepts and laws which are consistent with and are a demonstration of his own nature. The values which prevail in the kingdom are those held by the king who governs it. Therefore, if we wish to understand the nature of the kingdom of God, we need first to seek to understand the nature of God himself. Paradoxically, one way to do this is to seek to understand the nature of his kingdom!

Even before Jesus was born, his own mother proclaimed the revolutionary nature of the kingdom her son was to inaugurate. Her words, uttered in response to the dramatic news of her pregnancy, are sung by choirs to the most beautiful musical settings. They are said or sung every week in churches of all traditions and colours. They ring with a clear note of hope and justice. Yet often, as with the Lord's Prayer, their power and content are lost. If this were not true, the Church throughout the world would be more radically different from and challenging to our cultures. I am referring to the words of Mary, commonly called 'The Magnificat'. The latter part of her song proclaims:

> [The Lord's] mercy extends to those who fear him, from generation to generation.
> He has performed mighty deeds with his arm; he has scattered those who are proud in their inmost thoughts.
> He has brought down rulers from their thrones but has lifted up the humble.
> He has filled the hungry with good things but has sent the rich away empty.[3]

Mary has realised that the coming of God's kingdom will challenge the status quo of our world. The new kingdom is markedly different from the old. Jesus did not disappoint this vision when he began to teach. In Chapter 5, we looked at the so-called 'Lucan manifesto', Jesus' sermon in the synagogue at Nazareth. We noted there that his audience was so overjoyed at his understanding of God's kingdom that they tried to throw him off a cliff. But it is in Matthew 5–7, the so-called 'Sermon on the Mount', that we have Jesus' clearest teaching about his kingdom. It is in these chapters that it is placed in sharpest contrast with the kingdom of the world.

> Blessed are the poor in spirit, for theirs is the kingdom of heaven.
> Blessed are those who mourn, for they will be comforted.
> Blessed are the meek, for they will inherit the earth.

> Blessed are those who hunger and thirst for righteousness,
> for they will be filled.
> Blessed are the merciful, for they will be shown mercy.
> Blessed are the pure in heart, for they will see God.
> Blessed are the peacemakers, for they will be called sons of
> God.
> Blessed are those who are persecuted because of
> righteousness,
>
> > for theirs is the kingdom of heaven ...[4]

Someone once said to me that Jesus must have been a nutcase if he really believed all this. 'The world just is not like that', he protested. He was exactly right. The world is not like this at all. But God's kingdom is. And those who claim citizenship in God's kingdom must demonstrate these values in renewed and changing lives of humble service and self-sacrifice. Jesus is not a nutcase. He is utterly realistic about the violence, injustices, routines and problems of life. But he also claims that the world does not have to remain like this. He is not a fatalist, paralysed by the apparent size and hopelessness of the task into apathy and impotent acceptance of the status quo. We can be changed. The world can be changed. Justice will be done. God will not be mocked. One day, the whole world will have to face this reality.[5]

ASPECTS OF THE KINGDOM

The great conviction of the Old Testament prophets was that, despite current appearances to the contrary, justice would be done. God had not abandoned his people. The oppressive tyrants running all over the ancient Middle East would not have the last laugh. They might enjoy their power for a short while, but they will one day discover that even they are subject to a higher authority. This conviction grew and developed over a period of time. It formed the bedrock for understanding the past and the present. It eventually became the hope of a future kingdom of justice and shalom, a society ruled by the Servant King, in which God's will would be done perfectly. It is important for us to see these three aspects of the kingdom of God, past, present and future, as being complementary and not contradictory.

Jesus talked about the kingdom of God having already come.[6] He also described it as being near.[7] He said elsewhere that it is within us.[8] But he also insists that the kingdom is yet to be inherited, awaiting his people in the future.[9]

The kingdom has come: In the incarnation, the kingdom came. In Jesus, God's will was being done (and being seen to be done) on earth. He cast out demons and healed the sick. He taught about the significance of his life and death. He contradicted the world and culture in which he lived. He was the ultimate evidence that God's kingdom was different and was going to love the old world into destruction. He inaugurated the new age. By his death and resurrection, he transcended death and opened the gate to a glorious future. The end time, the future reign of God, has invaded history and given us a taste of what is to come. History has become meaningful, and we now live in the presence of the future.

The kingdom has not yet come: So far, we have had only a taste of the kingdom; it has not yet come in all its fullness. Three analogies might help us understand this. (a) When the Allies landed on the French coast on D-Day and established a firm bridgehead on continental soil, the end of the Second World War was in sight. But it took many months of continued fighting and suffering before the Allies could reach their goal. The war was won, but not yet won. (b) I remember seeing a football match in which one team scored nine goals. The game could have been finished at half-time, for it was clear that the opposition stood no chance of winning. But the game still had to run for ninety minutes. And, incidentally, the opposition still fought on as if they could win the match. (c) When I got engaged to Linda, I promised myself to her. We began to plan for our future together. We had to wait another three years before we could marry and consummate what had actually already begun. The kingdom is something like that: the victory of Christ has been won, the king has deposed the powers of this world, the end is in sight. But the drama still has time to run before it reaches its final conclusion.

The kingdom will come: Before Jesus faced his executioners he told his bewildered friends that he was going to leave them. He promised them that when he had gone he would send his Spirit (the encourager, who stands alongside them and pleads their case when they stand accused).[10] His Spirit would help them understand all that had happened and would equip them to face the uncertain future that lay ahead of them. Through the power of his Spirit they would turn the world upside down and would be a sign of God's kingdom here on earth. They would be the body of Jesus, continuing the work he began. But this would not go on for ever. The day would come when history would reach its conclusion. Jesus would return to establish his kingdom for ever and justice would be done. History, therefore, is neither aimless nor random.

There are some Christians who become obsessed with the future and spend much time and energy compiling timetables for the end times. Some seem to know more than God himself about when, where and how Jesus will bring the whole show to an end. Martin Luther had the right idea when he said: 'If I knew that Jesus would return tomorrow, I would still plant my apple tree today'. We are called to get on with the job of being the body of Christ on earth today, not wasting precious time speculating about God's timetable for the future.

THE KINGDOM AND THE COMMUNITY

We began this chapter by looking briefly at the Lord's Prayer. It is significant that Jesus responds to the disciples' request for teaching on prayer by underlining their community. He does not teach them to pray, 'My Father ...'. His model prayer begins by assuming that we come to God not as isolated individuals, but as a new family, a new community. This is a feature of the whole prayer and of much of Jesus' teaching. There is corporate confession ('Forgive us our sins ...') and a corporate commitment to forgive others. Jesus never simply addressed individuals as if they could somehow belong to him without being committed equally to other believers.

In the Sermon on the Mount,[11] Jesus addresses a group of his disciples and talks about their corporate life and witness in the world. The obsessive individualism of the modern Western world was unknown to the Hebrew mind. He goes on in Matthew 5 to say that his disciples are to be salt and light in the world. They are to be a living demonstration of the new age of God's kingdom, not just in their individual lives but in their corporate life together. They are a community of people whose common life, relationships, mutual service and sacrificial love shine like a fiercely burning light on top of a hill. They are to be noticeably different from other communities.

One of the things that is most difficult to come to terms with in any church is the diversity of the people there. There are always people with whom one would prefer not to associate. The church is a ragbag of motley saints and sinners. It is a multicoloured, multiracial and multicultural community which, despite all its weaknesses and failings, is called to demonstrate the power of God's kingdom on earth. Members of the Christian family do not have the luxury of choosing their brothers and sisters. They are chosen for us. My brother, with whom I have nothing else in common, is my brother. And I am called to love him and serve him and worship with him anyway. We are both called by the same Father. This is very different from the kingdom of the world, where one might expect to choose one's own company according to one's own likes, dislikes or interests.

As a student of German politics, I have always been fascinated by the rise of Hitler and the legacy he bequeathed to succeeding generations of Europeans. The most potent symbol of division our world has seen was the Berlin Wall (although this has been superseded, perhaps, by the obscene wall that currently divides Palestinians from some of their own lands and people). This artificial barrier was erected almost overnight on 13 August 1961. Germany's division seemed permanent. Families were suddenly separated, and a community was ripped in two. Beyond the obvious politico-military reasoning for this partition, there was a popular lack of comprehension as to how and why this could be done to a community. When the Wall was breached in 1989, the world rejoiced at the sight of reconciliation, reunion and the banishment of fear.

But the symbolism remains powerful. There are 'Berlin Walls' throughout our world, but most of them are not made of concrete. There is the wall of racism, which divides people according to their colour, race or country of origin. There is the wall of sexism, which separates men from women and turns either into a commodity. There is the wall of religious bigotry, which burns fear into communities in all parts of the world. There is the wall of social and economic class, which divides rich from poor. But Christian hope emerges from the conviction that Jesus

Christ has demolished these walls. In his new kingdom, there is no place for these barriers and divisions.[12] There are no arbitrary demarcation lines. Those who respond to the call to repent and to enter the kingdom of God have no excuse for rebuilding the walls Jesus has, by his life, death and resurrection, demolished. 'You are all children of God through faith in Christ Jesus, for all of you who were baptised into Christ have clothed yourselves with Christ. There is neither Jew nor Greek, slave nor free, male nor female, for you are all one in Christ Jesus' (Galatians 3:26–8).

THE SURPRISE OF THE KINGDOM

Why, then, are all churches not like this? Why do so many Christian communities offer only a very pale reflection of this new kingdom? Why do Christians perpetuate these divisions and even invent new ones? If the Church is supposed to be the great new community, what has gone wrong? The answer is found in the basic premise of this book so far: that Christians are weak people who need forgiveness and transformation. Sometimes Christians forget this and appropriate the truth they have discovered as if it were *their* truth. When truth becomes a weapon of power, it has been corrupted. But we must acknowledge that the most the Church can claim to be is a sign of the kingdom of God – it is not co-terminous with the kingdom. The Church ought to be the evidence for God in the world, wherein people can see a humble and open people being transformed into God's image. But the kingdom will be at work even outside of the confines of the Church institutions.

Jesus talked of people 'inheriting the kingdom'. I believed for many years that it is the people who believe the right things about Jesus who will inherit the kingdom.

However, there was always a dichotomy between *belief* and practice. Along with many Protestant Christians, I believed that we are 'saved by grace through faith', 'justified by faith' alone. 'Works', I believed, have nothing to do with salvation. I still firmly believe that we are justified by faith and saved by God's grace alone. But Paul has to be held together with James and Jesus. James makes it clear that if there is no practical evidence of faith, then there is no faith.[13] Faith is not just cerebral. No works, no faith. Someone who claims to be a Christian and shows no evidence of a changed life or changing priorities might well be deceiving himself.

For Jesus, love of one's neighbour is a crucial test of the reality of one's faith.[14] Jesus' understanding of love is never merely theoretical or emotional; he would simply not recognise a love that was purely sentimental. For him, love is immensely practical. In Matthew 25, he tells a remarkable parable about God's pleasure with those who loved in action and his displeasure with those who only pretended without realising that was what they were doing. Jim Wallis has referred to this chapter as his 'conversion chapter'. Reading it drew him back to faith, for it convinced him that God was passionately interested in real-life issues of poverty and justice – despite appearances to the contrary in the Church's priorities.[15] It is a chapter which is dramatically arresting in its forthright challenge to our culture's way of seeing both Jesus and other people.

Having divided the peoples of earth as a Palestinian shepherd would separate sheep from goats before nightfall, the King addresses those he favours using startlingly rich language. Those with whom he is pleased are invited to receive their proper inheritance, 'the kingdom prepared for you since the creation of the world' (verse 34). The criteria the King goes on to use to judge the world are not a new idea: they have always been part of the essential nature of God, even before anything was created. This kingdom has long been awaiting the time when those who have loved the King practically might be entrusted with it.

There are two factors to notice here. Firstly, the kingdom is an inheritance. An inheritance could not be claimed or demanded as of right. The father in the story of the Lost Son (Luke 15) does not *have to* agree to his younger son's request for his share of the inheritance. A father had first to give his blessing to his sons and choose who should inherit what. But the important fact is that it is the father's to give. He could choose to do something else with his estate. He is not obliged to hand it on automatically to his sons. Therefore, an inheritance is *conferred freely* by the father and is received in trust by the son. In this parable from Matthew 25, the righteous people cannot claim or demand the kingdom; they can only receive it as a freely offered gift.

Secondly, as we noted above, the criteria for qualification are intensely practical. 'For I was hungry and you gave me something to eat, I was thirsty and you gave me something to drink, I was a stranger and you invited me in, I needed clothes and you clothed me, I was sick and you looked after me, I was in prison and you came to visit me' (vv. 35, 36). No mention here of watertight doctrine, correct modes of worship, or correct ecclesiastical order. Love is not a doctrine to be possessed, examined or analysed. It is not just a matter of having loving ideas or inner attitudes. Love is to be lived. To bear the name of Christ and yet to love only when it is convenient or comfortable is to deceive ourselves and to perpetrate a gross hypocrisy. Calvary love is not selective and does not have favourites.

The biblical message is clear: we are invited to respond in faith to God's grace and love. We become disciples of Jesus and open our hearts and minds to radical challenge and change. If our minds and our values do not become conformed to his, if there is no practical evidence of faith in changed relationships and changed lifestyle, then we have not even begun to understand or experience his grace. If we claim to be lovers of God, but neglect others and live selfishly, then we must agree with the conclusion that we have not comprehended one iota of Jesus' gospel.

Returning to the story, the righteous are welcomed by the King. But they are surprised at his congratulations and do not understand his judgement. For when they fed the hungry and clothed the naked, they did not do so with the ulterior motive of gaining extra points in heaven. They loved practically, irrespective of the response. For love cannot be other than ruthlessly practical. They were not aware of having tended the needs of the King and are surprised by his full identification with those in need. The King reassures them that in serving the needy, in exercising simple, sacrificial love, they have done God's will and loved him. They are evidence of the truth of the Beatitudes. And God welcomes them.

It is quite shocking, then, to consider the other people who do not receive the King's inheritance. They, too, are very surprised. They have probably loved and worshipped God. They have probably been keen on defending their fine theological understandings against the errors of others. They have possibly 'moved on in worship', singing the right songs and adopting the correct postures. Perhaps they have seen the beauty of liturgy and the rehearsal of services as the most important thing in life. They possibly have enjoyed fellowship in the Church. But it has not made any difference to the world they inhabit. There is little to distinguish them from the culture in which they live. Their values are the same, but with a veneer of religiosity on top. Perhaps they have thought that loving God was a private affair which could be carried on independently of others. Perhaps they loved other Christians, but isolated themselves from the needs of those who did not belong to the Church. Perhaps they saw Christian activity as an end in itself, rather than as a means to a greater end: maturity, holiness, sacrificial service of all God's people. Whatever the case, they have misunderstood what it means to love God by loving those made in his image.

Their sudden realisation is horrifying to them, for they did not recognise in the needs of others the face of God. 'When did we see you hungry or thirsty or a stranger or needing clothes or sick or in prison, and did not help you?' The implication is that if they had known it was the King who was in need, they would have done something about it. It comes as a terrible shock to discover that God is not impressed with that attitude. The love recognised as that of the kingdom of God is an indiscriminate and uncalculating love which pays no attention to convenience or reward. It is a fierce love which freely denies self, embraces the leper, forgives the enemy and does not set itself up as judge of others.

PARABLES OF THE KINGDOM

One of the things which can afflict many of us is the desire to have everything defined. We want a clearly defined doctrine of everything, with no loopholes and with every t crossed and every i dotted. It is a great frustration to many of us, then, that Jesus does not oblige us with clearly formulated and structured definitions of the nature of the kingdom. He never says, 'The kingdom of God is ...'. Rather, he says time and time again, 'The kingdom of God is like ...'. He then gives an incomplete picture of what the kingdom is about. He invites his hearers to use their imagination in trying to understand or visualise the kingdom. Why does he do this? (And isn't it a bit risky?)

The kingdom of God is dynamic, not static.[16] It is like a mustard seed, which is tiny and grows into a large and useful tree. It is like yeast, which grows and spreads through all the dough. It is like hidden treasure, which is found by someone who risks everything in order to possess it. It is like a net, which is used to sort out who belongs to the kingdom. It is like a very generous landowner and employer.[17] All these stories involve action. They show that God is generous and just. His kingdom belongs to things which begin very small and grow imperceptibly into things which are large and fruitful. If I saw a mustard seed, I would probably not even recognise it as being a seed with potential for life and growth. Yet it is this apparently insignificant and tiny seed which is likened to the kingdom of God.

This ought to be extremely encouraging. Many of us have a very low opinion of ourselves and our gifts. We know what we are really like and find it hard to grasp that God loves us and accepts us as we are. But he takes a long-term view of us. He says that the kingdom belongs to such as us, for we have no delusions of grandeur. We are small. He will nurture us until we slowly grow. Like yeast, he will use us to pervade the dough of the world, making it grow and come alive with taste. The kingdom will grow within us and we will grow within the kingdom.

Jesus is thoroughly realistic about us. He knows our weaknesses and potential for failure. He knows we are small and insignificant. And that is all he needs from us. If we present ourselves to him as a fully-grown tree or a ready-baked loaf, there is not much he can do. We begin small, and we need not pretend to be other than we are.

PETER'S STORY

One of the most encouraging characters in the Bible is Peter. There are others like him in the Old and New

Testaments who loved God powerfully and knew how to sin wholeheartedly, too.[18] But Peter was Jesus' friend. And if I had been Jesus, I would never have chosen Peter to be my disciple – let alone the one on whom I was to build my entire future church. Peter comes over as a big man in all respects. He is big in stature, able to do a demanding physical job at sea. He has a big opinion of himself and his loyalty to Jesus. He has a very big mouth, which lacks a filter from his brain. He frequently misunderstands Jesus. He pledges total allegiance to Jesus, whatever the cost to himself, but ends up a weeping wreck of a man, hiding away, disillusioned and disappointed with himself.

In Matthew 26, Jesus is eating his final meal with his friends. They have not understood his warnings about his impending death. Once again, he refers to what is about to happen. Clearly he is tense, anticipating the torture that lies ahead of him. He knows that, when he needs them most, all his friends will desert him. He tells them that this is what will happen. Peter leaps to his own defence: 'Even if all fall away on account of you, I never will' (26: 33). Jesus tells him that even he, Peter, the Rock, will deny him three times. But Peter is adamant: 'Even if I have to die with you, I will never disown you' (26:35). The other disciples agree.

Jesus does not despise Peter for his bravado. He knows that Peter will not be strong enough, but he does not jump down his friend's throat and accuse him of imminent cowardice. He accepts Peter's allegiance in the spirit in which it is offered. He is not going to humiliate Peter or charge him with not having a very accurate self-image. He lets him be.

Peter's lesson is a hard one to learn. He learned a lot about himself that night. He could do no other than drop his image of the big self-assured man. He had failed miserably, and he could not avoid the fact. He was a broken

man. What possible use could he be to God now? Imagine
what he must have been feeling: self-hatred, fear, shame.
After all, he has committed the worst possible sin in the
book: he has disowned Jesus in public.[19] What hope is there
for him? Surely God will be angry and reject him as a
useless failure.

According to John's account (21:15ff.), the crucified
and risen Jesus goes out of his way to refute all this. He
does not recriminate Peter. He does not say 'I told you
so'. He does not remind him of his failure and weakness.
He does not make Peter feel small. He does not question
Peter's suitability to hold positions of responsibility in the
Church because of his past errors. On the contrary, Jesus
invites Peter to reaffirm his loyalty. This time, Peter is not
deluded about his own power and ability. His loyalty is now
realistic and humble. Jesus calls him to take responsibility
for the other disciples, to feed them and teach them. Jesus
reinstates Peter lovingly in full awareness of what Peter was
like and what he had so recently done.

Now, if that is not encouraging enough, the story continues. Peter went on to lead an extraordinary life as a
leader, preacher and teacher in the early Church. He continued to be Peter, stubborn and narrow-minded. In some
cases he was able to learn; in others he was not. He fought
with Paul and, no doubt, continued to fight with himself.[20]

That is the stuff out of which the kingdom of God is
made. It is the raw materials of ordinary human beings
who respond to the call of God. It is a kingdom full of
people who know their need and their weakness (often
learned through great failure or hardship). It is a kingdom
of hope, for it is rooted in a God who takes us as we are
and changes us beyond our wildest imaginings. John Bell's
song[21] is a fitting prayer with which to conclude. And it is
a prayer to be made by Christians who know they are not
alone, but part of a new community.

1. Take this moment, sign and space;
   Take my friends around;
   Here among us make the place
   Where your love is found.

2. Take the time to call my name,
   Take the time to mend
   Who I am and what I've been,
   All I've failed to tend.

3. Take the tiredness of my days,
   Take my past regret,
   Letting your forgiveness touch
   All I can't forget.

4. Take the little child in me,
   Scared of growing old;
   Help him/her here to find his/her worth
   Made in Christ's own mould.

5. Take my talents, take my skills,
   Take what's yet to be;
   Let my life be yours, and yet,
   Let it still be me.

7

HOPE IN THE DESERT

A desert is a dry and barren place. It recognises the extremes of heat by day and cold by night. It can be fruitless and lifeless; little grows there. There is little expectation of change. A desert is a lonely and seemingly endless place, infertile, inhospitable and frightening. It smells of danger and death, of hunger and thirst.

However, this is the judgement of someone whose experience is of urban life on a densely populated island in the northern hemisphere. Here there are fresh vegetables in the shops, a profusion of colourful and satisfying fruit, packets and tins of all descriptions. There is an almost infinite variety of goods and experiences at our disposal: television, theatre, cinema, music, dance, education. Existence can be rich and choice wide. The climate is moderate (i.e. the rain is warmer in summer than it is in winter), the environment offers surprise, adventure, colour, excitement, diverse smells and tastes. Our expectations of lifestyle, diet, culture and experience know no bounds. A visiting nomadic Bedouin would be bewildered, disorientated, frightened and lost here.

It is easy to think of our rich (relatively) Western urban experience as normal. For the Bedouin, it is extremely abnormal. In fact, such a visitor to our society might make some shrewd and unwelcome observations on what we rather euphemistically call 'life' in the Western world. For him, the desert is not an infertile and inhospitable place to live. It is not a place of death. It is home, a place of life and culture.

If I were to go tomorrow to an African desert, I would have to make a very important choice: either to run away from it, seeing it as alien, dangerous and evil, to be avoided at all costs; or to embrace the new experience, learn from it and live it. In the desert, I would experience much that could not be experienced anywhere else. I would learn of a new relationship with the land and the environment. I would experience total silence and total darkness, experiences which are almost impossible to enjoy (or endure) in our modern technological society. I would learn a new appreciation of heat and cold, of the power of the sun and the moon. Even the stars would look different. I would have to learn where to look for food, although the unfamiliarity of the environment and what it offers might be off-putting. I would be able to learn about solitude and the sense of insignificance in a big universe. I would have to get used to not knowing the world news on the hour every hour. I would be experiencing a new reality, a game played according to very different rules. If I was sent into the desert, the world – my world – would look a very different place.

The desert is not alien to the world, even if it is alien to my own limited experience. It is a truism that a desert is not a jungle, a tropical rain forest, or a city. But it is not somehow wrong because it is not one of those. It is a very real part of the real world in which we live and move and have our being. To describe our world to a visitor from another planet without mentioning the desert is to be economical with the truth. It is to be dishonest, to misrepresent reality, to live in a pretend world.

Human experience of life is like the world we inhabit. There is the fertile jungle (with all its hidden dangers as well), the polar icecap, the developed urban sprawl (with its variety of cultural opportunity). But there is also the desert, where our experience might be one of sterility, barrenness, aridity, lostness, fear, depression, frustration, loneliness, hunger and thirst. For Christians to deny this element of our existence is to be dishonest and unbiblical, as we shall go on to see later.

Some people choose to enter the desert. They seek solitude, or want to withdraw from the rush of a busy life. They fast and pray and keep silence. They might deprive themselves of material comfort in order to help themselves to order their priorities. Some forms of retreat can be like this.

There are others among us who perhaps ought to enter the desert, even if the prospect is a fearful one. Perhaps others can see that we need to slow down and stop for a while, withdraw from the busyness and order our lives anew. We might need to learn afresh how to listen to the 'still small voice' of God reassuring us of his love, mercy and guidance.

However, most people who enter the desert do so involuntarily. They do not wish to be there and have not chosen to go. They have not prepared for the different climate and lifestyle. They can find themselves horrified at their new environment, afraid, bewildered, confused, and feeling rejected. It is this most common type of experience which I want to address here.

AN UNSOUGHT-FOR DESERT

At the ripe young age of nineteen, I went to live and work in a beautiful area of southern Germany. A requirement of my university course in modern languages was that I had to work for six months in Germany, followed immediately by six months in France. These months away from home proved extremely significant for the future direction of my life and ministry.

I had gone off to university in Yorkshire as an enthusiastic and active evangelical Christian. I soon became Evangelism Secretary of the Christian Union and led the organisation of an evangelistic mission – the first at that particular university for many years. However, there was some vociferous opposition to the mission from within the Christian Union. Opposition and suspicion from outside the Christian family did not come as a great surprise; but opposition from within took me aback, and I did not come out of the conflict unscathed.

This experience of conflict (and my rather bad handling of it), coupled with the natural strain of seeing the mission through to its conclusion, certainly took its toll. Soon afterwards, I had to go into hospital for an operation. Physically, I felt weak and tired. Spiritually, I felt empty and abandoned, disillusioned and confused. I was faced with a terrible dilemma: either to acknowledge the situation and my questions about God, or to avoid the challenge to my beliefs and pretend I was the strong Christian of my public image.

This all happened in February 1978. In the March, I set off on the long train and boat journey to Schwäbisch Gmünd, where I was to live for the next six months. At my work (freelance technical translation), I was successful. I made friends with a wonderfully generous and open family who lived nearby and attended a small church in the town. Yet, if anything, my sense of isolation, loneliness and depression simply worsened as day followed day. I was desperately homesick, physically run down, and I missed my fiancée badly. I longed for the props which had so successfully supported my Christian faith in the past. My longings to recapture my experience of the past went unfulfilled.

Many evenings I would return from my work in a village nearby and go to bed very early. I would lie there, wanting the anaesthetic of sleep, asking God where he was, imploring him to make himself real once more. Often I would weep with anger and frustration. I could no longer be sure that God was even there; perhaps I had been conned after all. This thought, and its implications, were chilling, but I had to respond somehow.

At the time, I believed that doubt was the manifestation of faithlessness. Therefore, doubt was to be avoided at all costs, lest God be angry with me for my lack of faith. Little wonder that a child once defined faith as 'believing things that you know aren't true'. I came to a position which, for me, was a very significant and crucial watershed in my own experience as a Christian: if God is not there, I cannot continue to bear the name of his Son. I felt I had no option but to proceed with integrity. For faith that could not face reality was a mere delusion. Faith that worked only when everything was fine was not faith at all. No longer could I leave God untested – especially intellectually. If he was sought and not found, despite the experiences of others, I would have no alternative but to cease to be a Christian and face the consequences of life in a world without God. This step of commitment was the first and most vital step in my finding God for real again. The walk through this particular desert lasted years, not days. And even then it did not end: it simply changed direction.

DESERT EXPERIENCES

Central to Francis Schaeffer's approach to Christian apologetics[1] was the idea that all of us have to reach the line of despair in our thinking and experience. This line is that point where we finally realise that we cannot live consistently with our views of God, ourselves and the world. Only when we reach that point with integrity can we begin honestly to search for truth and the reality of

God. Why? Because only then can we truly see our need and our weakness and therefore act with genuine humility and integrity.

This element of despair is a feature of the experience of many people in the Bible. Yet these experiences were never purposeless, random, accidental or outside of God's involvement. In fact, as we shall discover, God frequently sent his people, those whom he loved above all else, into a desert.

ADAM, EVE AND THE FAMILY

When we meet Adam and Eve in the early chapters of Genesis, they are introduced to us as the pinnacle of God's creation. God has created all that is, and he loves what he has made. Not only is it good, it is ideal. Nature is in harmony with itself, humanity's relationship with his world, his Creator and his fellow woman is perfect, and God is pleased. The man and the woman are the jewel in the crown. They reflect the Creator: they are moral beings, able to reason and think critically, free to choose to love or not to love; free also to live with the responsibility for and consequences of their choices.

Then, despite all this, their curiosity gets the better of them and Adam and Eve choose to exceed their place in the creation order. When God asks them to own their deeds, they immediately attempt to shift the blame. Their instinct is to protect themselves at the expense of the other and to avoid responsibility and accountability. They experience shame and embarrassment, and know that they have lost something irreplaceable: complete trust and a relationship which was transparent in its love, freedom and integrity. Adam and Eve hide from God, an impossible task if ever there was one. God comes looking for them and finds them. They must face their responsibility. Their life has to change radically in all respects. From now on, life will be a struggle. They are expelled from Eden.

As is the case in most families, their children are very different in temperament and personality, and this leads to conflict. Cain is jealous of his brother, Abel. In a fit of jealous rage, Cain slaughters his brother in a field. Like his parents before him, Cain discovers the inconvenience of having to answer to a God who is consistent in love and justice. Cain's selfish disregard of his brother's worth demands a response. He is sent away to build a new life elsewhere.

It is interesting that, according to the story, Cain leaves God behind and chooses to live away from him. It is as if he wants to live as though God does not exist and has no claim on his life. The first thing Cain does is to build a city and call it Enoch. In Chapter 2, we noted the question raised by Cain's action and looked briefly at one theologian's answer.

Jacques Ellul suggested that Cain's actions paint an accurate picture of what every human being does. When we take our leave of God and live our lives without reference to him, we are forced to create our own world. This world, with its limits and parameters, offers us meaning and security. We build a 'city' and surround it with a protective wall. This limits our vision of the world, but gives us a place and an identity. Furthermore, it provides us with a framework for understanding where we fit into the world. It gives us a clearly defined territory and makes us feel that we matter.

What often seems to happen, though, is that our efforts at constructing our 'city' (possibly done unconsciously) crowd our minds and affections, thus preventing us from recalling what we have lost. We busy ourselves to death. And the walls which are designed to afford us security in fact become the very barrier which blocks out the light.

Our experience and our view of the world become limited and our sight becomes narrow and dim. We think that our own small world is the ultimate meaningful reality. We confuse the flimsy construction of our artificial city with the total reality of the universe. It is little wonder, then, that life can become a pursuit of the unattainable, a rat race for meaning and significance, an effort to avoid facing the big questions about God and the real world.

However, history also tells us that city walls have a habit of either collapsing or being breached. We might well consider fortunate those cities whose walls crumble under the invasion of reality or despair. This is not as perverse a thought as it might first appear to be. For, when the walls come tumbling down, we can see how flimsy they actually are. We can suddenly catch a glimpse of a world and a reality that is much bigger than our little city. Once again, we can see the light and perceive distant horizons which were previously obscured. Our own 'city' is put in perspective. The defensive walls, designed to give security and comfort, give way to a world of colour, variety and vast opportunity.

To continue the analogy, the real tragedy occurs when circumstances lead to the destruction of our city walls and we cannot stand the light. All too often, new walls are quickly constructed to replace the old ones. And the illusion of meaning and security is perpetuated. The light proves too disturbing, too threatening. The exercise of responsibility demanded by the open new world appears too frightening, and we prefer the mock security of walled darkness. After all, we knew where we were when it was dark.

When we encounter God and he lifts us out of our little world and opens to us a whole new universe, our experience is always going to be uncomfortable, threatening, challenging. Leaving the city behind and walking out into the new world might feel very risky and reckless. But we can do it with confidence because he has done it first. As we saw in Chapter 4, Jesus is the pioneer of our faith; and we do not walk anywhere that he has not already been. The alternative is to retreat into the mock safety of our own little city and block out the light. Of course, blocking out the light means that the warmth is also blocked.

A RANSOMED PEOPLE[2]

Circumstances have constrained the people of Israel to migrate to the more fertile and prosperous Egypt. Their survival demands it. But, as often happens to immigrant communities in an alien culture, the natives have become increasingly restless. The immigrants seem unable to control themselves and keep having more and more children. As their numbers have grown, they have become perceived increasingly as a threat to the authority, identity and security of their Egyptian hosts. Motivated by fear and suspicion, the Egyptian authorities decide to put the immigrants in their place. And so the screw has begun to be turned, and life for the Israelites has become very hard. Their erstwhile hosts have turned them into slave labour and are busy exploiting them, exhausting them.

Under this oppression, exploitation and suffering, the Israelites begin to face up to difficult questions. Their existence as an identifiably distinct people owes itself to the conviction that God has promised them blessing, prosperity, land, and the special favour of his loving presence. But where is Abraham's famous God now? He promised blessing – but the present reality is suffering and oppression. He promised prosperity – and the result is poverty and hardship. What use is a God who cannot even defend his own people? Perhaps Cain was wiser than we had originally thought, after all.

A reluctant hero, Moses, along with his easily-led brother, Aaron, plagues Egypt's leaders with God's demand for justice and liberation. After some dramatic persuasion, the authorities give way. The Israelites go free and flee the land of their suffering. However, the method of liberation is both unorthodox and unpleasant. It involves smearing blood on the doorposts and lintel of each house in order that the inhabitants might be recognised as belonging to God and therefore be spared the death of their first-born.

So, in this way, the Israelites are offered freedom. But they are offered only one way of achieving it. No blood, no freedom. Otherwise freedom would exact a very heavy price: the death of the eldest son in the family. The point is that the people can go free, but they cannot choose their own method for achieving that freedom. God does not always make salvation comfortable, convenient, clean or even happy.

Having enjoyed the sweetness of vindication and liberation, it might have been nice if God had thrown a big party and left them to celebrate and enjoy their new-found freedom. But God knows of what we are made and, instead, leads them into a desert. Is it not bizarre that God, a God of love and power, leads his liberated people into a desert, a place of scarcity and severity of experience? Yet this is precisely what God, in his wisdom, does. And the question 'why?' is a very good one to ask.

Being set free is one thing; using that freedom is another entirely. The people's liberation is only the beginning of their journey, not the end. The party can wait until the destination is reached and the journey is ended. Like a baby, newly delivered from its mother's womb and traumatically thrust into a strange, bright new world, the people have to learn and grow and change. And they quickly prove themselves to be not very good at any of those three.

Clearly, God did not see any inherent value in keeping them in the desert for so long. It was the people's stubborn unwillingness to learn the truth that condemned them to such a long sojourn there. This was a sort of judgement on the people; that is to say, if they could have grasped the truth after a week, they could have entered their promised land sooner. The fact is, however, that they did not and could not.

It was vital that the Israelites learn some crucial lessons. But these lessons could not be learned in the Promised Land. The conditions necessary for them to be able to learn were not comfortable ones. They were to be deprived of a great deal. They were to endure suffering, frustration and doubt. They were to face the unknown in a strange environment – and learn what really matters in life.

The essential lesson they had to learn was that 'man does not live on bread alone, but on every word that comes from the mouth of the Lord' (Deuteronomy 8:3). Kosuke Koyama, a Japanese theologian, has observed on this: 'This was an extremely important lesson for his people to know and understand before they went into the land of Canaan. God decided to spend forty years to teach this one lesson! … If God decided that he would use forty years, the subject of the lesson must be of great importance in his view.'[3]

For Israel, the experience in the desert was not just helpful, it was vital. It was absolutely essential. Life is more than food and consumer goods, physical health and cosmetic beauty, income and financial security. God, his values and words are more than necessary if we are truly to be free and live, for they reveal to us the truth about God's character and person. But there are no short-cut, easy ways to learn the lesson. There are some lessons that can be learned only in the desert. The Israelites had to learn the hard way that God's wisdom is more trustworthy than our convenience.

Koyama points out that a wilderness is 'an open space in all directions. It is a place full of possibilities ... But at the same time this open space is a dangerous, desolate space inhabited by demons and evil spirits ... The wilderness is thus full of promise and full of danger.'[4] In the wilderness, choices have to be made; priorities and values must be established. In the wilderness, we are stripped of all that is familiar and comfortable. In the wilderness, we are confronted with the starkness and fragility of our existence. We can either walk on, determined to face this truth and allow our lives to be changed by the experience; or we can simply spend the time complaining and hankering for the 'bliss' that was Egypt. Even past affliction offers a certain security. When in danger, romanticise the past.

Koyama beautifully expresses the nature of God's walk with us in the description of him as the 'Three Mile an Hour God'. In the desert place, we have to stop running, stop being hyperactive, stop flapping about in all directions. We are reduced to walking pace. We have no option but to slow down. The wonder of it is that when we do so we discover that that is the pace at which God has been proceeding all along. While we were racing round in frantic circles of activity, God was just a blur outside the windscreen. Now we are with him and he is walking alongside us. Now we are able to listen and learn and walk with him. Now we can cease the whirling pursuit of significance and simply be with God.

GOD IN THE DESERT[5]

Jesus has left the securities of home, family and job, and has embarked on a public itinerant ministry which he knows will have a sticky end. At the outset of this new ministry, Jesus comes to John, a recognised prophet, and asks to be baptised. John declines, knowing that he ought to be coming to Jesus for ministry. However, Jesus insists that John baptise him there and then in the River Jordan. He knows that his identification with his people, with all their failure, weakness and hard-heartedness, is to be complete. As he emerges from the water, a voice is heard from heaven. Whether anybody else present heard the voice or not is unknown, but Jesus heard it. The voice said: 'This is my Son, whom I love; with him I am well pleased' (Matthew 3:17). Now, this is made up of two quotations: Psalm 2:7 and Isaiah 42:1. Psalm 2 is a messianic psalm, affirming the kingly nature of Jesus' rule. Isaiah 42 introduces the 'Servant' theme, which culminates in the staggeringly beautiful 'Suffering Servant' of Isaiah 53.

This compound quotation is neither accidental nor random; indeed, it is extremely significant. Right at the outset of the ministry that will lead to a cross and an empty tomb, Jesus is faced with kingship of a radically different nature from that which might be expected of a great cosmic ruler. His kingship is not the powerful political status so much desired by Simon the Zealot and Judas Iscariot. Rather, his kingship is to be characterised by servanthood. And servanthood means not claiming one's rightful power and status, but rather laying oneself down for the sake of others. This paradox would have been immediately obvious to witnesses of the event and the original readers of Matthew's Gospel. But Jesus' friends were very slow to grasp the point, and the Gospels record Jesus' occasional impatience with their inability to get the message.

However, having had his ministry and mission clearly affirmed by God at his baptism, it might reasonably be assumed that Jesus should simply get on with the job of preaching, healing and forgiving people their sins. But that is not what happens. Once again, the wisdom of God confounds our assumptions. First, God's Spirit leads Jesus out, away from the comfort of the familiar and the kudos of public affirmation, where easy resolutions can be made, and has him fast in the desert for forty days and forty nights. Why does God lead his own Son out into the desert at this point and in this way? Surely Jesus needs encouragement, not hardship? After all, Jesus must be a safe bet for reliability anyway; he is God incarnate. The answer to these questions has important implications for our view of Jesus.

Christians affirm that Jesus is both fully human and fully divine. That is the biblical understanding of his nature and identity. Yet many of us find the latter easier to comprehend than the former. But if Jesus was fully human, and was tempted in every way as we are (as the writers to the Hebrews state so confidently),[6] then this episode in the desert was essential. For here Jesus is to be faced with real dilemmas, not theoretical or hypothetical choices made from the comfort of a distant armchair. In real situations of temptation, he has to choose whether he will walk the path of the servant or the powerful, dictatorial king.

It should come as no surprise, then, that the Satan attacks him where he is most vulnerable: 'If you are the Son of God, tell these stones to become bread'. What Satan is saying here is: 'Jesus, you do not need to hunger. You do not need to be materially deprived. You can fulfil your kingly duties *and* accrue all the material benefits along the way as well. If God is your Father, he will want to make life easy for you, not difficult. So why not just take a short-cut and change these stones into bread? Go on! You can do it. It won't hurt anybody. You don't need to suffer in any way; just compromise a little. Be reasonable, and don't be so hard on yourself. After all, remember who you are.'

Jesus knows he is human and must feel acutely the attraction of consummating his humanity by material satisfaction. The temptation is powerful. But servanthood means sacrifice, deprivation and the knowledge that human beings are spiritual beings who can afford even to lose life and still win. Jesus replies: 'It is written: "Man does not live on bread alone, but on every word that comes from the mouth of God"'. Jesus chooses God's way, the way of self-sacrificial servanthood, and rejects the costless way of easy compromise.

Nevertheless, Satan is not easily put off. He tries again, this time coming at Jesus from a slightly different angle. The chink in the armour, if there is one, is surely to be found here. He invites Jesus to throw himself down from the highest point of the Temple, knowing that God could save him. 'Jesus, look at the world below you. It can all be yours, without any suffering on your part. You know that if you throw yourself from this great height, God will command his angels to save you. Of course, that is if you really *are* the Son of God ... go on, prove yourself. Prove God! And, in case you want me to reinforce the point, I'll quote from Scripture to back up my invitation. Now, if it says so in the Bible ...'

Jesus must have found the temptation a powerful one. After all, who in their right mind would willingly opt for suffering and pain, especially if they had the power to avoid the same? We cannot help but wonder whether the hint of doubt, with its taunting sarcasm (*'If* you are the Son of God ...'), hurt his pride, challenged his own identity, or compelled him to prove the point. Jesus responds by saying that he is not there to perform miracles just to prove a point. He is not a performing monkey in a circus. He does not have to rise to the bait, swollen with pride, and play the devil at his own game. He does not have to conform to the devil's own methods: performance and the superficially miraculous. 'Do not put the Lord your God to the test', he replies. He is clearly choosing obediently to walk the way of suffering if necessary and will not take comfortable short-cuts. He is declaring his kingship to be one of self-sacrifice, servanthood and full identification with his people.

But, as is his nature, Satan is resilient and decides to have one more go for now. 'Jesus, you can have status and power: political, economic, social and religious. You name it, you can have it. You can have wealth and all that goes with it. Just play the game according to my rules. Do it my way. Accept my values, compromise a little, don't take it all so seriously, avoid the struggle. What's more, Jesus, you can have it all now, without any delay.' It really is the ultimate in 'taking the waiting out of wanting'.

Once again, Jesus adamantly refuses to take the easy way. He refuses to abandon the values of the kingdom of God, wherein power, success, wealth and worship look very different from their glittering form in Satan's hands. Jesus will not worship wealth, success, image, beauty or power. Jesus prefers to walk in God's way, even if doing so is long, hard, costly and excruciatingly painful.

Faced with real human dilemmas, Jesus has chosen his kingship. He has chosen the way of the servant. He has spent time in the desert, perhaps even unsure what God was doing with him there (forty days is a long time when nothing seems to be happening). He has faced the heavy cost of loving obedience to his Father, convinced that nothing matters more than walking God's way. The world will end, but God will not. Now he is ready to embark on his unique ministry. And, as this particular time of trial ends, Jesus experiences the relief and joy of having been faithful to his Father. Angels minister to him. He knows the closeness of God.[7]

JOY IN THE DESERT

Surely it goes without saying that the desert experiences recounted above were not easy to live through. But they were all necessary. It is frequently the case that God's refining work within us (both individually and corporately) makes particular progress during such times. God might seem absent or distant. We are aware that we are at a crossroads and must choose which way to go. The veneer of piety is stripped away, and we are left alone in the desert with God.

The desert experience, therefore, is not one to be resisted or avoided at all costs. We do not need necessarily to escape from it or despair of it. If we find ourselves in the desert, it can be a sure sign not of God's abandonment (though it might seem like it) but of his guidance and love. For he is wiser than we are, and he knows what we need. God, who loves us, will not hesitate to lead his children into a desert if that is where they need to be. If he led his beloved Son into a desert, he shall also lead us into a desert. We shall emerge into a promised land only if, or when, we have learned what it is God is trying to teach us. Even the Promised Land has its own deserts, famines and faults. He is usually trying to teach us to depend on him and value nothing more than him. He is teaching us to worship him alone, to love him and find genuine, lasting security in him alone. Seen in this way, the desert experience is one to be embraced, endured, explored, accepted and learned from.

Some friends recently recalled a speaker at a missionary conference using an image which was very helpful to them. They had suffered greatly in many ways during their missionary work in an African country. They were at a point of despair, all but longing to give it all up. The conference speaker pointed out that there are flowers and plants which grow only in the desert. They cannot be found in a jungle or fertile area. It is facile, therefore, and a recipe for frustration and disappointment, to look in the desert for the familiar plants and flowers we have known in the past which only grow in fertile areas. To seek earnestly plants which do not grow where we are, even if we have seen them grow beautifully elsewhere, is a waste of time and energy. It is a doomed exercise and must be avoided. Past experiences and enjoyment of such plants must be left behind. We are to move through the desert (at walking pace) and look with fresh eyes for the tiny and unique plants which grow only in the desert. There we will discover God's creative life where we least expect it. The surprise can be marvellous and life-changing. For God is a God of such surprises.

POSTSCRIPT

At the beginning of this chapter, I recounted my own experiences in Germany. It took several years of searching before I recovered any sort of spiritual equilibrium or direction. I graduated from university, married, worked for four years as a linguist at GCHQ in Cheltenham, and then went to a theological college in Bristol to train for the ordained ministry in the Church of England. Six months before ordination, I once again found myself in a desert. Intellectually, I was thriving, and God made more sense than ever before. Philosophically, Christianity was consistent, and I was prepared to argue apologetics with anyone. But God himself became increasingly distant. I had a crisis and called out to him. My cries were met with silence. I spent a weekend in tears, unable to eat or sleep properly. I sought advice from people I knew to be wise and trustworthy. I longed for God, but knew I could not just live in the past. It is not too dramatic to say that my faith, my job and my future were at stake here, for I could not be ordained as a minister unless something changed.

In the midst of my grief, I wrote the following entry in my private journal on Friday 20 March 1987:

I cried tonight. I don't often cry, but when I do I seem to do it properly. My eyes feel tired and sore now. I feel as if I've let the world leak out and I can never be the same again. I had to cry; I couldn't help it. No reason, no intention; just a deep, deep grief, which, like antifreeze in a car radiator, always finds any weak spot through which to escape. It's not easy to feel desolate, empty and sad, sad, sad. But for me it is very necessary. For there seems to be so much inside me which hides, lies, pretends and corrupts that I need to get it out into the light of day, the light of Christ, and cry it onto the cross. I don't want to understand it, or learn from it, or rationalise it; I just want to get completely rid of it and, by handing it over to the crucified one, share in his resurrection life and light.

I need to know God and experience his love and warmth. I cannot carry on with my suppressed doubts and deep fears that I am being conned. God must prove himself, or I can't carry on. I cannot be a minister of a gospel I assume to be right, but of which I have no experience.

I think I cried because I reached the end of a road and I can see no way ahead in my dark night. I need more than a map – I need a co-driver, a navigator. I need God tonight more than I need anything in this whole world. What will I do if nothing happens? If he keeps silent and distant? I'll keep seeking and searching. But I'll probably cry again. And again.

You must please turn my mourning into dancing, for I've never danced like I should. I'm not sure I even know the music. Please sing it to me while I sleep and help me to enter your rest. I must know God. Nothing else matters right now … Don't turn me away. Please.

A few days later, I was helped to understand something of why I was finding this experience so difficult to handle. A wise tutor at my college showed me how my professional training and work had taught me to rationalise everything. I liked to be in control of myself, my emotions, perhaps even my relationship with God. Yet in this desert I was decidedly not in control. The experience was fearful. And, ultimately, the deliverance was as gentle as the despair was powerful.

I cite the above example from my own experience simply because it was transforming and fruitful. I did not enjoy it. But the turning point was the decision to face up to my doubts and fears and let God be God.

The Bible is full of examples like mine. Knowing God can be painful. He can lead us into the desert. It should teach us to seek him above all else, with a thirst and a hunger we have never known before. The Psalms of the Old Testament reflect the whole of life: the abundant expression of joy and confidence in God, and the expression of complaint, fear, abandonment, confusion. It is clear that our worship must be thoroughly honest. For God knows our heart and is not deceived by sham praise. The root of joy, the route to God, is often found in the desert. Whether we experience it or not depends on whether we embrace the experience or run away from it.

> As the deer pants for streams of water,
>   so my soul pants for you, O God.
> My soul thirsts for God, for the living God.
>   When can I go and meet with God?
> My tears have been my food day and night,
> while men say to me all day long,
>   'Where is your God?'
> These things I remember
>   as I pour out my soul:
> how I used to go with the multitude,
>   leading the procession to the house of God,
> with shouts of joy and thanksgiving
>   among the festive throng.

121

Why are you downcast, O my soul?
    Why so disturbed within me?
Put your hope in God,
    for I will yet praise him,
    my Saviour and my God.
My soul is downcast within me;
    therefore I will remember you
from the land of the Jordan,
    the lights of Hermon – from Mount Mizar.
Deep calls to deep
    in the roar of your waterfalls;
all your waves and breakers
    have swept over me.
By day the Lord directs his love,
    at night his song is with me –
    a prayer to the God of my life.
I say to God my Rock,
    'Why have you forgotten me?
Why must I go about mourning,
    oppressed by the enemy?'
My bones suffer mortal agony
    as my foes taunt me,
saying to me all day long,
    'Where is your God?'
Why are you downcast,
O my soul?
    Why so disturbed within me?
Put your hope in God,
    for I will yet praise him
    my Saviour and my God.[8]

HOPE IN THE FACE OF DEATH

During my time as a university student, I worked for a while in Paris. In my spare time, I got to know the city very well. One place I was interested to see was the cemetery at Père Lachaise. It covers a huge area and contains the graves of many famous people, including Oscar Wilde, Chopin, Edith Piaf, Jim Morrison and many heroes of the French Revolution. Some graves are covered by simple slabs. Others are attended by statues or busts. Others are housed in enormous and elaborate buildings. There are monuments to people who, in their lifetime, had fame and fortune. These stand side by side with memorials to victims of Nazi genocide in Europe, particularly in the concentration camps.

As I rounded one corner, I was confronted by a group of people kneeling on the damp autumnal ground. Some seemed to be praying or meditating. Some were weeping. One woman, probably not more than twenty years old, was arranging the many flowers on top of the tomb. Chopin had been dead for many decades, but the place where his body returned to dust had become a shrine, a place of reverence and worship.

On this particular afternoon, the cemetery was full of people. It was one of the most popular stops on the tourist trail in Paris. A coachload of camera-waving foreign tourists poured off their bus like air escaping from a bursting balloon. Chattering and laughing, they arranged themselves with expert dexterity in front of the monument to the victims of Auschwitz. After a barrage of clicking shutters, they raced back to the bus, the doors closed and they went on to the next photo opportunity on their tour. I guess they had 'done death'.

Death is fascinating. It is possible to stand and look at a grave for hours. Death makes us stop and think and wonder. Children who experience bereavement ask candid questions about what it is like to be dead, and often it is the interrogated adults who find it difficult to cope with the questions. This is ironic because death is the ultimate shared experience. The death of each individual has a social context.[1]

Different cultures and faiths approach death in different ways, and some ways are healthier than others. But few are as unhealthy as what has been termed 'the Western way of death'. It is ironic that it is in the technologically sophisticated West, where God has allegedly been displaced by science and reason, that death is so badly handled. Or perhaps it is not so ironic, after all. We can land a man on the moon and send space probes to other galaxies; we can perform miracles in operating theatres and remove all physical strain from cooking, cleaning, working and travelling; computers shape our lives; we are drunk with the unchallenged assumption that progress is an absolute good; and the ultimate affront to progress and scientific genius is human death. It is an obscenity in the minds of people who see no meaning in life other than the transient significance they arbitrarily attribute to it. Death is the enemy. We cannot control it.

The visual media and the entertainment industries provide us with death at every turn. Dozens of deaths happen on our television screens every day, and most of these are brought about violently. But they are instant and sanitised – and we do not live through the experience of those bereaved. John Donne's conviction that 'no man is an island' is implicitly rejected. Television death concerns individuals whose death is forgotten as instantly as it happened. On the news, we do not see the real brutality of death and violence, only the sanitised and edited account which is deemed suitable for our tender sensibilities. It is as if the audience is not to be upset by reality. The plethora of death in the media is presented in such a way as to parody the real experiences of death and bereavement. It actually prevents us thinking too much about the reality of death.

Martin Heidegger, the German existentialist philosopher, was right when he said that the whole of life is a 'being towards death'. Death is inevitable, the only certain fact of life. It challenges our way of life and our understanding of what life is all about. The way we think about and approach our own death will determine how we live our lives and what our priorities and values will be. The reality of our hope will be tested ultimately by the phenomenon of death. Questions about God and meaning can often be ignored when life is good and busy; but the unwelcome intrusion of death or bereavement drags the issues before our eyes and demands a response.

WHAT ON EARTH HAS HAPPENED TO DEATH?

Two events witnessed many years ago have stuck firmly in my mind. One is the televised funeral of Mrs Indira Gandhi after her assassination; the second is one of the first funerals I conducted after my ordination. They show quite graphically the contrast between two cultures and their way of dealing with death.

I had never seen a Hindu funeral before, and I knew very little about Hinduism. Whilst watching the news on television one evening, I was presented with pictures of thousands of people thronging around the open coffin of Indira Gandhi. The procession followed her as she was taken to her funeral pyre at the edge of the River Ganges. The commentator informed us that it was Hindu custom for the family of the deceased to build the pyre, to dress the body in ghee butter, for the eldest son to circle the corpse several times before setting light to his own mother's body. Then the film cut to this very scene. My initial (and ridiculous) reaction was one of disgust. How could he set light to the body of his own mother? Where were the funeral directors?

The significant thing here was the degree of involvement by those bereaved. They all took a physical part in the funeral. It was a family and community affair in which all had a part to play. Death was a fact of life, however tragic the circumstances of the death might have been. It was a phenomenon to be faced and addressed. Mourning was institutionalised, and there were rituals to accompany this process.

One of the first funerals I conducted as a curate in the north of England left me bemused. Many funerals are attended by very few people, often only immediate relatives if there are any. Very occasionally, only the undertakers attend. But at this particular funeral there were approximately one hundred in the congregation. After the woman's death, her body was removed by the undertakers. *They* tended the body and made it presentable. *They* dressed it and laid it in the coffin. The family's involvement was limited to agreeing to the type of coffin, the venue of the funeral and the hymns to be sung. No one wanted to take part in the service other than to be there in the congregation. A large number of young people attended the service in church. What struck me, apart from the lack of family involvement, was the fact that the younger people seemed embarrassed. They seemed to avoid looking at the coffin (which greatly surprised me). When, during a hymn, I caught the eye of a young man in his twenties looking at the coffin, he quickly looked away. After the funeral and interment, the younger people were apparently embarrassed and reluctant to talk to me.

Now, I am aware that there may be very good reasons why people do not wish to be spoken to by the clergyman. There are many good reasons why mourners might not wish to expose themselves by publicly reading the Bible during the service. But this experience, though by no means universal, is far from unique. Death is hard to confront, especially for young people who never see it or touch it, who are optimistic about the lives they have stretching out ahead of them. But the experience left me with many questions about how our culture deals with death.

Philippe Ariès had a very interesting book published in 1974 entitled *Western Attitudes Toward Death*.[2] In this book, he traces changes in attitudes from the Middle Ages on. It is not possible to do justice to his thesis in just a few lines; but, with a very broad brush, this is the picture he paints.

In the Middle Ages, people prepared for death, and death was a very simple thing. There were rituals to accompany death and the process of dying (for example, lying with an eastward posture). The dying person was in control of proceedings and presided over its ritual. It was a public ritual that involved parents, children, friends and neighbours. In contrast to the fearful taboo of today, death was familiar and, to use Ariès' description, 'tamed'. Aries claims that, for more than a millennium, up to the end of the seventeenth century, people had been as familiar with the dead as they were familiarised with the idea of their own death. Death was something that was seen, smelled, touched and talked about by the whole community. It was seen as part of the order of nature, not a blasphemous rupture from it. Death was not to be escaped from or glorified, it was simply natural. But the imminence of death made life worth the living.

According to Ariès, the shift in attitudes can be seen in the developing individualisation of sepulchres. There were changes in the rituals surrounding death and dying, with death increasingly becoming seen as a rupture with the natural course of life. In the nineteenth century, death and passion combined in a Romantic eruption of ostentation. Death was accepted with greater difficulty than in the past.

From the early Middle Ages through to the mid-nineteenth century, changes in attitudes towards death were slow. But, according to Ariès, in the latter half of the twentieth century we witnessed 'a brutal revolution in traditional ideas and feelings'.[3] In the USA, the United Kingdom and the industrialised countries of northern Europe, death became shameful and forbidden. Only now is this creeping into the Latin countries of central and southern Europe. The truth about death was beginning to be hushed up.

As medical technology has advanced, so has responsibility for one's death been removed from the one who is dying. Now the power lies in the hands of those who decide whether or not to inform the person of the truth of his or her condition. This shift is brilliantly described in Tolstoy's *The Death of Ivan Ilyich*,[4] in which a dying man is scared by his ignorance of what is happening to him. But all those around him refuse to address the fact of his imminent demise. It is as if there is an unspoken conspiracy.

Between 1930 and 1950, attitudes changed very quickly and markedly. The location of death shifted from the family home to the hospital (where the 'patient' often dies alone). This means that all the rituals surrounding the process of dying and death, which previously would have been observed within the security of the home, are banished.

Death is a technical phenomenon obtained by a cessation of care ... Death has been dissected, cut to bits by a series of little steps, which finally makes it impossible to know which step was the real death ... All these little silent deaths have replaced and erased the great dramatic act of death, and no one any longer has the strength or patience to wait over a period of weeks for a moment which has lost a part of its meaning.[5]

Now the focus of attention is on the bereaved. An 'acceptable' death is one which is acceptable to the survivors. An unacceptable death is one which causes survivors embarrassment. It evokes strong emotions, and these are to be avoided. Emotion is to be expressed only in private.

Traditional public and communal rituals of mourning have now all but disappeared – apart from the creation of public shrines where the 'unexpected death' took place: at the side of a road, on a bridge, or (in the case of Princess Diana) the whole of Central London. There are still residues left in those close communities (such as the Irish Catholic or African immigrant communities) of our cities. In many rural communities, there is still opportunity to see the body, a social obligation to attend the funeral and the party which follows it. But these residual phenomena do not negate the power or validity of Ariès' analysis.

'WHEN I DIE I ROT'[6]

So said Bertrand Russell, the famous mathematician and atheistic philosopher. For him, death is the end of everything. Nothing has any real objective meaning anyway. We live ... and then we die. That is all there is to it. However, most people cannot be as dispassionate about death as Russell wants to be. The fact that they believe their life to have intrinsic value leads them to conclude that there must be more to life than death. If life is without any objective value, why should I see death as an enemy? Why are we so afraid of death? Why does it render so many understandings of life futile? Why does it ultimately matter?

The American Declaration of Independence states unequivocally that 'all men are created equal and independent, that from that equal creation they derive rights inherent and inalienable, among which are the preservation of life, and liberty, and the pursuit of happiness'. Now, happiness might be a commendable state of being, but our culture has made it into a god. And the trouble with death is that it cuts across happiness and spoils the party. It strips away the veneer of image and exposes reality. Ariès puts it like this: 'On showing the least sign of sadness, one sins against happiness, threatens it, and society then risks losing its raison d'être'.[7]

It hardly needs saying that the rich capitalist world has seen an unprecedented (and quite horrific) escalation in the amount of money spent on youth culture, the beauty and fitness industry, food fads, cosmetic enhancement and so on – and all this in a world in which two-thirds of all people are poor and hungry and relatively unconcerned about their wrinkles. The rich world is obsessed with staying alive, avoiding age and pain, venerating beauty, manufacturing false ideals of superficial glamour. Modern health technology, treading a fine line between a search for ethical absolutes and the pragmatic equation (whereby what is possible is legitimate), is a two-sided coin: it allows a few to live, because of complex and expensive treatment, whilst allowing many to die from preventable diseases. Somewhere, our priorities have gone awry. So has our ability to cope with life and death in a meaningful way.[8]

It is all very well to analyse and criticise our culture for its inability to cope with the reality of death, but how is one to think of death realistically by way of constructive response? If death has become the 'pornography' of the twenty-first century (as Gorer describes it),[9] how can it be re-appropriated and the taboo be removed? We must begin with an understanding of the nature of human mortality and the inevitability of death.

MORTALITY AND MAN

I am mortal. Today I am alive and breathing. I can smell, taste, see, hear, feel and move. But I have no guarantee that this state will continue. By this evening, I could be dead. My heart could stop its beating rhythm, my brain could cease to function. I am mortal. From dust I have come, and to dust I shall return. I have no reason to doubt or question the desirability of my death; it is simply a fact. I will die.

The Anglican Funeral Service is very clear and realistic about the nature of our mortality. Quoting from 1 Timothy 6:7, it affirms the fact that 'we brought nothing into the world, and we take nothing out'. At the point of committal at the graveside or in the crematorium, we read from Psalm 103:

> The Lord is full of compassion and mercy: slow to anger and of great goodness. As a father is tender towards his children: so is the Lord tender to those that fear him. For he knows of what we are made: he remembers that we are but dust. The days of man are but as grass: he flourishes like a flower of the field; when the wind goes over it, it is gone: and its place will know it no more ...

Physical death is real because our bodies are made of chemicals which have a limited life. However strong we are, we are still frail. It does not take very much to kill a man, really. We are like grass that blows away in the wind. We are like flowers which bloom, bursting with life and colour, only to wither and die and disappear.

But that is not all we are. We are not just physical entities, whose existence ends when the body expires. In the creation narratives in the book of Genesis, God breathes his life into the body of the human being.[10] We are spiritual beings, more than the sum total of body and brain. We are living beings, capable of making relationships and experiencing emotions. We can think and reason, laugh and weep, cultivate and kill, worship and pray. And God knows how he has made us. He is not surprised by death. Neither is he horrified by it.[11]

RESURRECTION AND HOPE

In Chapter 4, we saw the incarnation as the key to hope in the real world. We noted that, if faith has any justification, it must be able to face reality and all the horror the world can throw at it. The wonder of humanity is not just that God created us in his own image. It is, further, that he came and shared the lot of his creation and suffered and died with us. The death of Jesus was real. His body was completely dead. He was placed in a tomb, and the tomb was sealed.

At that point, hope was an empty word. People like Mary Magdalene, who had found meaning and hope in the person of Jesus of Nazareth, were devastated. The future, which had looked so bright, now looked dark as night. Crucifixion on Friday had killed off any vision for the future and made present events seem meaningless. But, by Sunday morning, the gloom had been exploded by the glorious and bewildering light of resurrection. The body of Jesus was no longer in the tomb. His friends began to meet him, speak with him, touch him, eat with him. Jesus was truly alive.

The fact of the resurrection[12] makes sense of the crucifixion. If Jesus had remained dead, all he had ever said and claimed and promised would have been empty and void. But in his resurrection he transcended death, rendering it impotent. No longer could it be seen as the ultimate enemy. Its sting had been drawn, its laugh had been silenced. No longer could death cock a snook at life, questioning its validity and meaning. Death itself had been defeated, and life took on a whole new dimension. The words of Jesus to his friend, Martha, resound with hope:

> I am the resurrection and the life. He who believes in me will live, even though he dies; and whoever lives and believes in me will never die.[13]

What without the resurrection would have been ridiculous has become the most powerful and reasonable truth in the world: anyone who shares in his death will be raised by that same God to new life with Jesus.

For the Christian hope is not just 'pie in the sky when you die', even if it has sometimes been presented as such. It is grounded and earthed in human history. God has never abandoned his people to the fate they so readily deserve. Jesus walked among us, suffered and died for us, and transcended death to assure us of the reality of eternal life. Death is not the end of the story; it is just another chapter in the plot. And the Jesus who has been through life and death assures us that if we will trust him he will lead us the same way. This is why the apostle Paul could say, honestly and without false piety or a desire to escape, 'for me to live is Christ, to die is gain'.[14] The best *is* still to come.

The Christian attitude to death, then, is not one of fear or dread. It is not one of resistance to the inevitable, but of acceptance of God's will. This is not fatalistic; it is realistic. For it is rooted in a Jesus who deliberately went to his death, knowing it was the only way to life. Jesus has made it possible for us to face death, that of ourselves and others, without fear. He sets us free to face death honestly and to die well. If this is true, it also means that we can be honest about our contradictory fears! We need not put on a show of bravery or piety. God is our Father, and he knows of what we are made. He knows our fears and our frailty. And he knows that death has lost its power, despite the appearance it maintains.

DERELICTION AND HOPE

For many of us, the prospect of our own death is less difficult to accept than the death of someone we love. If I die, I am the subject; it is happening to me. I will not be left behind to have to cope. But if it is my husband, wife, child, parent or friend who has died, then I have to experience a complex of emotions and questions. I might be left with a great deal of work, sorting out the affairs of the deceased. Bereavement is so desperately painful that sometimes we wonder how we can sustain it. The suffering it causes can be extremely powerful.

It is no surprise, then, that bereavement renders us very vulnerable. Faced with the stark reminder of our mortality, we find ourselves asking what actually turn out to be religious questions: What is *my* life really all about? Is there a God? If God exists, where is he and what is he like? Why does this death hurt so much? Why does it matter? Where is he/she now? These questions (and there are many others) penetrate to the heart of what it means to be human, made in God's image. But, if we wish, we can ignore or suppress the questions and busy ourselves into a state of inertia.

Extensive pastoral experience of other people's bereavement has taught me a great deal about the necessity for honest thinking about death. There can be nothing worse than the sight of a bereaved Christian trying to put on a show of unmoved faith purely in order to maintain the image. Conforming to other people's expectations is not always a good thing, especially when the hidden, unconscious agenda is to spare other people the embarrassment of having to cope with your emotions and grief. When Jesus arrived at the home of a friend who had recently died, his response was to weep and be angry with death.[15] Grief, and its proper expression, are essential. If the pressure of genuine grief is not expressed appropriately, it will find some other way out.

The experience of bereavement is one that can be seen as a gift, for it helps to put the rest of life and its priorities into a right perspective. The pain has to be worked through as a community, although the Western elevation of the individual makes this difficult. Perhaps we need to invent new social rituals to express (and allow expression of) the powerful emotions generated by bereavement. It is not a contradiction to be sure of the death of death itself and to grieve and mourn for someone we love and miss powerfully. Equally, it is not inconsistent to fear the process of dying and the terrible social ruptures caused by death, whilst at the same time embracing a trust in a Jesus who has transcended death. One element in our mortality is, after all, the difficulty of accepting that mortality. It is not a sign of Christian weakness, or lack of faith, to experience the paradox of simultaneous fear and trust.

SUFFERING, DEATH AND HEALING

The last twenty or thirty years have seen a growing re-emphasis on the healing ministry in our churches. This has resulted partly from an increased openness to the power of God and the renewing grace of his Holy Spirit. The various manifestations of the charismatic movement have been greatly used in blowing fresh air into the lives of individuals and churches that had lost sight of God's reality. New gifts have been discovered and a new joy in worship experienced by many people. A greater trust in a God who is immediate and active has led to an increased sense of expectation. But the expectation of the miraculous, particularly in relation to healing, has also thrown up many conflicts and inconsistencies. Does God heal? Does he want us to suffer? Why are some people healed and others not? Is suffering inevitable? What is the link between my suffering and my sin? If I were faithful to God in every respect, would I stop suffering? I am tempted to point straight to the incarnation again: Jesus, the Son of God, chooses to go to a cross. Suffering and death are not an end in themselves, but they are the ineluctable way to life. Jesus does not run away from suffering, as he did not run away from the desert. He embraces suffering and removes the need to fear death. Helmut Thielicke, a German theologian who preached and pastored his church through the bombing of Stuttgart during the 1940s, wrote:

> Jesus Christ did not remain at base headquarters in heaven, receiving reports of the world's sufferings from below and shouting a few encouraging words to us from a safe distance. No, he left the headquarters and came down to us in the frontline trenches, right down to where we live and worry about what the Bolsheviks may do, where we contend with our anxieties and the feeling of emptiness and futility, where we sin and suffer guilt, and where we must finally die. There is nothing that he did not endure with us. He understands everything.[16]

He is the pioneer who has gone before us and promises to take us with him.

This is not to glorify suffering or to ennoble it. Suffering is dreadful and is confined to our fallen world. It can be divisive and destructive, but it can also be redeemed. My fear is that Christian claims and demands for physical healing often have less to do with faith and openness to God's will, and more to do with a refusal to accept our mortality and inevitable death. Why should God heal my cancer or my cold? Will I trust him even if I die?[17] The greatest expression of faith has to be the willingness to accept that God, in his eternal wisdom, knows better than I do what is for the best. He is sovereign. And he has spent the whole of history trying to convey to us that life does not end at death; that eternity is real. The incarnation has God opting into mortality and suffering, not exempting himself from it.

Christianity has at its heart the conviction that it is the whole of the human being that matters. Her physical ailment has to be seen in the context of the whole. In Mark 2:1–12, Jesus is in the town of Capernaum teaching the crowds who have followed him home. There is a scraping in the roof above him, as if the ceiling is being picked away. Eventually, a hole appears and the daylight streams through. The crowd beneath is not only covered in dust, but is also astonished to see four men lowering another man through the roof. This man is paralysed, and his friends have been unable to get him through the crowds to meet Jesus. One would expect Jesus to take pity on the man's plight and heal him on the spot. After all, the faith of his friends ought to be rewarded and encouraged. But Jesus does not oblige. Instead, he says, 'Son, your sins are forgiven'.

Frankly, if I was that man, that is not the message I would want to hear. My sins can be dealt with any time; it's my legs that need dealing with now. But Jesus is not stupid, and he knows that by forgiving sins he is making an explicit claim to be God. For, as the people well know, only God can forgive sins. But this man also needs to know that

God loves him and accepts him – to acknowledge the fact that he needs more than his legs healed.

Well, Jesus goes on to heal the man's body as well. But he has made his point very clearly: you can have the best health possible, but if you do not know your need and have the liberating experience of God's forgiveness you can never be truly free or truly whole. The corollary is, of course, that it is possible (and possibly it is the norm) to have a body which displays its mortality and frailty and yet be a whole person. William Barclay has put it like this: 'The man who knows he is within the [salvation/healing] of God knows that he is "safe when all safety's lost". It is the conviction that nothing in life or death can separate him from the love of God.'[18]

Janani Luwum was Archbishop of Uganda during the tyrannous reign of Idi Amin in the 1970s. The probability of his being murdered by Amin's soldiers was real, and he did not run away from it. Two months before he was killed, he said this:

> I do not know for how long I shall be occupying this chair. I live as though there will be no tomorrow. I face daily being picked up by the soldiers. While the opportunity is there, I preach the gospel with all my might, and my conscience is clear before God that I have not sided with the present government, which is utterly self-seeking. I have been threatened many times. Whenever I have the opportunity I have told the President the things the churches disapprove of. God is my witness.[19]

For Christians like Luwum – and there are many – suffering, whether it be from illness or persecution on account of their faith, is not something to be avoided at all costs. Death has lost its power, its sting drawn by the risen Jesus Christ. This is why Dietrich Bonhoeffer's last message to his friend, Bishop George Bell, spoken as he was leaving for his execution at Flossenbürg, said: 'Tell him that for me this is the end, but also the beginning'.[20] Bonhoeffer would have agreed with the statement of John de Gruchy, a South African Christian, who wrote: 'Christian discipleship is a response of freedom and love to the suffering love of God. It is becoming caught up in the passion of God.'[21]

DYING WELL, LIVING WELL

We observed at the outset of this chapter that our approach to life will partly be determined by the way we face our own death. When we come to terms with, and are at peace about, our own death, we will have the freedom to see clearly what life is all about. The inevitability of death and the fact of our accountability to God will help us order our priorities. Life will take on a whole new complexion. For it will be enjoyed, not as an inconvenient prelude to eternity, but as the beginning of the experience of eternal life here and now.

Hope in the face of death presupposes that we first acknowledge the reality and implications of our mortality. It is a hope that is rooted and grounded in the transcending power of the risen Jesus Christ over death. It is not a vague hope, based only on religious wishful thinking. Rather, it is a hope which is based on historical events and yet which is appropriated by faith. Jesus is the key to the future, as he is the key to the past and present. To trust in him is to be set free from fear. To experience his forgiveness and love is to be able to face death knowing that heaven has already begun.

TRANSFORMATION

Jesus' disciples were bemused by his predictions of his own death. They could not understand it. If Jesus was the

Messiah, how could he possibly die like that? How could he do so much good and still be rejected by people? Had he not come to save them? If he could not save himself, surely he could not possibly save anybody else. As we noted earlier, they were devastated by his torture and execution; bereft and horrified, they hid and wept. Their world had all but ended, and the future looked very bleak.

But their confusing encounters with the risen Christ changed them. I imagine their bewilderment continued: after all, it is not every day that you meet someone who was once very dead and is now very alive. Jesus taught them to await the coming of his Spirit in power. The Holy Spirit would help them understand and make some sense out of all that had happened to them and around them in the last three years or so. So they began worshipping and praying together. On the day of Pentecost, the Spirit came in great power and transformed them. People who had been hiding for fear of suffering the same fate as Jesus became bold and open about their faith. One reason for this is that the reality of the resurrection of Jesus from the dead and the experience of his continued presence within them dispelled their fear of death. Nothing the world could throw at them could remove Jesus from them.[22]

History teaches us that the early Christians suffered dreadful persecution, and a number of Jesus' immediate disciples suffered eventual execution. Their faith did not preserve them from suffering. On the contrary, it was the direct cause of their suffering. But they were changed people, empowered to face death without fear and to live life to the full. Their conviction was that of Paul:

> What, then, shall we say ...? If God is for us, who can be against us? He who did not spare his own Son, but gave him up for us all – how will he not also, along with him, graciously give us all things? Who will bring any charge against those whom God has chosen? It is God who justifies. Who is he

that condemns? Christ Jesus, who died – more than that, who was raised to life – is at the right hand of God and is also interceding for us. Who shall separate us from the love of Christ? Shall trouble or hardship or persecution or famine or nakedness or danger or sword? As it is written:

> 'For your sake we face death all day long;
> we are considered as sheep to be slaughtered.'

No, in all these things we are more than conquerors through him who loved us. For I am convinced that neither death nor life, neither angels nor demons, neither the present nor the future, nor any powers, neither height nor depth, nor anything else in all creation, will be able to separate us from the love of God that is in Christ Jesus our Lord.[23]

HOPING AND PRAYING

Several years ago, I was visiting a prison regularly and became acquainted with a number of inmates. I remember asking one man, who was approaching the end of a life sentence for murder, what hopes he had for the future after his release. I actually asked him what he hoped for. He replied with a list of things he wanted to do, places he wanted to see, things he wanted to buy, and people he wanted to meet. It was the stuff of which dreams are made. Whilst driving away from the prison later that afternoon, I became convinced that I had asked him the wrong question. By asking him what he hoped for, I had inadvertently encouraged him to think in terms of what he would like to happen. I ought to have asked him what he hoped in. The distinction between the two questions is very important.

The last few years have seen a number of challenging conflicts in the world: the first Gulf War, Chechnya, Bosnia and Kosovo, the invasions of Afghanistan and Iraq. Before the last invasion of Iraq, which led to the downfall and eventual execution of Saddam Hussein, millions of people marched and campaigned for peace, hoping against hope that war and bloodshed could be averted. But any hopes for a quick or 'surgical' strike have been left embarrassed by the quagmire of violence and horror visited upon both Iraqi civilians and the occupying forces.

I have a strong memory of the time before the first attack on Iraq after Saddam invaded Kuwait. While the crisis in Iraq was brewing, the newspapers and broadcast news bulletins were full of foreboding. My children were quite young at the time, and I was concerned about their fears. One evening, my eldest son could not get to sleep and came downstairs. He was crying and appeared very worried. He was only eight years old, and he was frightened that there would be a war and that we would be caught up in it. My wife and I attempted to soothe him and allay his fears. I then heard myself saying to him, 'Don't worry, if there is a war it won't affect us; we are a long way from Iraq. We will be all right.' This line of thinking was successful in getting my son back to bed and off to sleep, but it was I who could not sleep later. My answer to his fears was totally inadequate and narrowly parochial. If I was an Iraqi Christian father, how would I have answered him?

A good test of our understanding of God and the validity of our theology is to subject it to the experience of other people. As a student of German politics and history, I was frequently puzzled by the prayers of Christians in my church for safety, prosperity and health – almost as if we would only recognise God's 'blessing' if everything was going well for us in our little world. These are marvellous things to enjoy, but whether the possession of them can always be seen as a sure sign of God's blessing is debatable. For many Christians around the world, their faithfulness and obedience to God lead them consciously into hardship, deprivation, persecution and death. These experiences can be horrible and cannot be romanticised. The dilemmas facing Christians in the Third Reich are a case in point.

Martin Niemöller, for example, was a pastor in an affluent district of Berlin at the time Adolf Hitler gained power. Though worried by the violence and by neighbours' disappearances, he only slowly became aware of the threat posed by Hitler. He eventually became outspoken against the Führer and helped establish the Confessing Church in Germany. In 1937, he was incarcerated in Moabit Prison, awaiting trial. Seven months later he was acquitted, but the same night was transferred to a concentration camp as Hitler's 'personal prisoner'. He remained in captivity until the end of the war. His letters, written during his time awaiting trial, are very revealing. He prays for his family's safety and longs for news of them. But he even sees their safety as secondary to the need for justice in Germany. For even faithful individuals are caught up in the suffering of the wider community as justice works its way through.[1]

Any understanding of hope must be capable of standing up to whatever history or events throw at us. The grounds of hope must be valid for all Christians in all parts of the world, whether their experience be easy or hard. A parochial hope might be convenient, but it will eventually disappoint. God must be capable of handling the rotten side of life as well as the good bits. A God who disappears into an embarrassed silence when things do not go according to the convenient Christian plan is no God at all. He is the figment of a frightened imagination and feeds on wishful thinking. Such a god is an idol, and idols need to be demolished, for they represent unreality. They represent a lie.

This is why the question I posed to the prisoner was inappropriate. He might be sorely disappointed by the eventual turn of events. His hopes might be dashed and his bitterness or fatalism increase. What he needs (among other things) is genuine hope. Hope, that is to say, in a God who makes sense of the past, gives courage for the present, and leads us into the unpredictable future. It is hope in the God who, though transcendent, has walked among us and experienced what we experience. It is hope in a God who, as a man, hangs on a cross and despairs

144

that God has abandoned him. And it is hope in a God who draws the sting of death by leaving a sealed tomb empty behind him.

HOPE FOR THE PAST

We have seen in the previous chapters of this book that the past is important. It can be said that I *am* my past. I am only what I now am because of all the people, events, decisions, successes and failures which have shaped me in the past. I come to tomorrow bearing the accumulated baggage of the last nearly fifty years. I cannot escape my past, for it has made me *me*.

For some people, this can sound like terrifyingly bad news. Mistakes that have caused much guilt and grief haunt the memory and prevent real peace of mind. It seems such a pessimistic view of life. It seems to condemn us all to relentless sadness, like being held on a carousel, unable to jump off. This perception is, however, perverse.

In the creation narratives of Genesis 1–2, God brings order out of chaos. Human beings seem very adept at turning order into chaos. History is the experience of God bringing order out of the chaos we produce; and the same is true of our individual lives. When I look back on my life, I am confronted by success and failure, sadness and joy, peace and turmoil, weakness and strength. I also see how ignorant I am about myself. The Bible presents a very good picture of this experience when it describes God as a potter and me as a lump of clay.[2] When a potter begins his work of art, he does so with a lump of shapeless earth. As he begins to shape the material on his wheel, he gradually smooths out the distortions. He does not just throw the clay in the bin and wait until he finds a lump that is already perfectly shaped. Rather, he blends the distortions into the substance and fabric of the completed work.

As well as glorious or unremarkable features, my past might display some horrendous bits. It would be nice if God were to lop them off and discard them. I could then forget them, and he would not have to look at their offence. Sometimes this is the way Christians present God's dealings with human sin: he simply wipes them out and throws them away. But this is only partly true. Indeed, God promises to cancel out my sin. But the consequences and marks of that sin go with me into the future. They must become part of the fabric that is me. What God does is to draw the sting of sin, set the experience into its proper place in my life, bring order out of the chaos. I am not just redeemed; I am a redeemed sinner. The wonder is not that I cease to be a sinner when I experience the forgiveness of God; rather, it is that I, a sinner, am redeemed.

To be forgiven is the most liberating experience known to us. It sets us free from the grinding power of guilt and opens us up to a hopeful future. It confers the right to start again. To be forgiven is not to ignore the reality of the past, but to acknowledge and embrace it and use it to move forward into the future. God's gift to us is to take the chaos we often experience and slowly to bring order out of the raw materials we are. I am my past. I no longer have to pretend to be what I am not. I no longer have to hide from the shame and embarrassment of past mistakes and wrong decisions. Hope is rooted in forgiveness and the possibility of being changed. For it enables us to look ahead without fear.

HOPE FOR THE PRESENT

In Chapter 6, we looked at Peter, Jesus' friend who swore he would stand with Jesus through life and death. We noted how he failed miserably (yet understandably) and fled the scene of Jesus' torture, his self-respect destroyed and his hope evaporated in a cloud of disillusionment and fear. It was a long couple of days before the resurrection. After Peter's encounters with the risen Christ, he obediently awaited the advent of God's Spirit at Pentecost. His life thereafter was changed beyond recognition. Peter was transformed into a man of hope, who lived in the present but in the light of the eternal. He knew from experience that the future might bring humiliation, suffering and death to him, but he also knew that there is more to life than what happens to the body.

Being grounded in the hope we have described in this book is literally revolutionary. For it enables us to see the present in the light of the eternal, that is, of what really matters. Fear of failure and suffering is mitigated by the assurance that life is not random but meaningful. Hope, then, is not just an attitude of mind; it is a way of life. It underlies our motivation, priorities and values and it shapes the way we face up to the reality of our experience in this world.

People who encountered Jesus went away different; they could never remain the same. In a very real sense, he provoked a crisis in their lives. He offered meaning and purpose, peace in the midst of a difficult world, love to the loveless. But he also made it absolutely clear that following him would not be without cost. Faith in Jesus is radical: it goes to the roots of our being. It is impossible to claim allegiance to him and, at the same time, to remain unchanged. Jesus invites change in our attitudes, in our values, and in our lifestyle. When we discover and experience the hope that is embodied in this same Jesus Christ, we will be willing to pin everything in life on him. We will trust him for both life and death. The reality of our present experience, whether good or bad, will not be able to move us from this sure and certain hope: that this same Jesus who lived and died among us, and who

147

appeared to his friends on the third day, is behind and present in the world now; that he is the beginning and end of all things; that he puts all the transience of this world into perspective; that he guarantees the coming of the kingdom of God.

In one of his most famous and challenging books, the young German theologian Dietrich Bonhoeffer wrote: 'When Christ calls a man, he bids him come and die'.[3] Bonhoeffer was not a fantasist – he died on the Nazis' gallows just days before the end of the Second World War. He knew that to follow Christ meant making decisions which might have serious consequences. Those who claim to belong to Christ, to be his friends and followers, must take seriously the importance of making decisions and living with the responsibility for and consequences of them. We have no alternative but to commit ourselves to living in the kingdom of God in the real world. Commitment is costly and frequently messy. It involves taking risks and not always being sure that it will all work out. A faith which inhibits the taking of risks is a dead faith. In fact, it is no faith at all. Safety does not require faith; life in the kingdom of God demands it.

The message of hope represented in this book is one which sets us free from the need to have everything carefully mapped out ahead of us. It is one which sets us free to be honest and open with God and with one another. It is rooted in a Jesus who knows us inside out and still loves us. He is not surprised by our weakness and failure. In fact, these are the foundations on which he builds faith which is without fear. In short, we have the freedom to risk much and make mistakes. We are set free to live life to the full, with Jesus at the heart of all we think and say and do. Hope for the present means freedom to live. For it is hope in a God of love and justice, who is utterly realistic about us and who will surprise us at every turn.

HOPE FOR THE FUTURE

When Jesus told his friends what would shortly happen to him, they did not understand. That is not surprising. But Jesus clearly was not surprised or shocked by their inability to grasp his meaning. He knew that, later on, the proverbial penny would drop and they would remember his words. Then they would realise that he, Jesus, was not taken by surprise at his arrest. He was ready to face his trial and suffering; he was not simply a prisoner of history capable only of reacting to events as they occurred.

It is this same Jesus who leads us into the future. We do not have a blueprint for our lives. We cannot say what will or will not happen to us. We cannot predict the future. But our hope can be rooted in the Jesus who has himself transcended death and inaugurated the coming kingdom of God. He has promised to return and usher in the ultimate new age. He leads us, with our redeemed past, through the present uncertainties, into a future of which he is the Lord. The hope we have and live out is one which looks the uncertain future in the face and walks into it like a man walking into a dark tunnel, knowing that his guide has not only seen the light at the end, but has tasted it.

Some Christians live as if they were already in some sort of private heaven, having little concern for this world and its problems. They think that the world is doomed anyway, but that they are redeemed and separated from the world. There are other Christians who are so passionately concerned to see the kingdom come on earth now that they lose sight of the eternal. Both are right and both are wrong. We live in the real world of the here and now. As followers of Jesus, we are committed to working for justice and peace. Our bodies are Jesus' body. Our hands and feet are his hands and feet, our voices his voice. But we are also passing through a world which is transient. Our eyes are fixed on the future kingdom which will bring an end to the injustices we experience here. We are citizens of another kingdom, and our primary allegiance is to another King. Our values are those of another place, and our life and service are seen in the light of the eternal will and character of God. Christian faith is both this-worldly and other-worldly, but the evidence of its integrity will be seen in our this-worldly commitment.

CELEBRATION

The life of the followers of Jesus must stand out against the status quo of the culture in which we live. For, as we have seen, disciples of Jesus have different values, see people in a different light, and serve people for different reasons. They are a community of ordinary mortal people who are united simply in their discipleship. They long to see the kingdom come to all people and all cultures. They strive to see the values of the kingdom shaping the lives of societies and individuals. They are a people prepared to serve others irrespective of race, colour, creed or status – and irrespective of response or reciprocation. They are a people who can celebrate the hope of the kingdom under the most adverse conditions. They can do this because they have tasted the power of forgiveness, reconciliation and hope and cannot turn back to the old patterns.

It is easy to pick out communities such as the Sojourners Community in Washington D.C. or the Iona Community in Scotland and show how they exist as servants to the people among whom they live. They choose to live on very little money, get involved with the weaker and poorer end of society, and, at the same time, joyfully celebrate the life in the kingdom of God. Most people, however, do not live in those sorts of communities. For them, the question is: *How do I live this life of the kingdom in my everyday realm of work, family, mortgages, interest rates, responsibilities, church and so on?* Jesus always began with the small, not the large. He took individuals who were very limited in their understanding and asked them to follow him. This meant gradually reversing some of their previously assumed values. For example, money had to become the servant of the kingdom, not its master. The desire for power over people was transformed into a commitment to serve, whatever the cost. Enemies were to be loved, not hated. The weak were to be protected and served, not discarded as unfit for survival. People were to be valued as God's creation; deference to social status as defined by wealth or success was to find no place in the Christian community.

The hope of such a church or community is to be celebrated. It is not a vague grasp of some intellectual concept which will help us to limp through life, somehow attributing an arbitrary meaning to an otherwise random existence. It is the powerful experience of God's love. It is the experience and expression of God's grace. It is rooted in forgiveness and reconciliation. It is passionate for justice and peace. Yet it continues to hold even when justice and peace seem remote and fanciful. Its principal expression at the heart of Christian worship is the Eucharist, a celebration not of blind optimism or fantasy, but a proclamation that Christian hope is grounded firmly in the historical events of incarnation, crucifixion and resurrection.

For many centuries, people have had to face very difficult questions about God. In the Bible, the psalmists articulate many of the genuine feelings of those who suffer and wonder where God is. *Why do the wicked prosper whilst the righteous suffer?*[4] *Why does God seem remote and indifferent when we need him most?*[5] The psalmists were good Jews. They knew that it was not only legitimate to be honest with God, but that it was absolutely vital. God is big enough to cope with our questions and frustrations. He is God the Creator who is not surprised by our anger and grief. He is a God who hates hypocrisy and loves truth.

When I was a teenager, I came to believe that I was to praise God in every situation. If disaster struck in any way, I was to summon up all my faith, thank God for the disaster and praise him. I tried hard for many years to be like this. However, I always had the niggling doubt that I was being dishonest and that God was not fooled. The day I realised that God is more interested in the truth of my feelings than in my artificial faith, I felt strangely liberated. God himself became more real and more like God. For I knew I no longer had to pretend to him. After all, God looks on the heart, not the outward appearance of the fine words of praise.[6] Who was I trying to fool? If God looks into my heart and mind and sees anger or frustration, what does he make of my statements of praise? The psalmists told God what they really felt and thought. They praised God, they complained to him, shouted at him, asked him difficult questions, took encouragement from God's help and presence in the past.

When God's people live, serve and worship together, they truly celebrate. For they have something worth celebrating: they have a God who, like a father, longs to know his children in all their experiences of life. He longs for them to be open and honest, to see that he is big enough to soak up the venom without returning it. This is what forgiveness is all about.[7] The community of hope is one which can celebrate its liberation from the need to pretend or conform. It is a community which allows its members to be honest and faith to be real. It does not suppress difficult questions or shun uncomfortable expressions of apparent faithlessness. It is a community which is, therefore, tolerant and loving, weeping together with those who weep and laughing with those who laugh. It is a community of people whose worship will be grounded in and reflect the whole of life's experiences. And it is a community of people learning, despite all its weaknesses and inconsistencies, to love.

GRASPED BY HOPE

It was suggested to me that I should not write this final chapter. A wise friend recommended leaving a number of blank pages at the end of the book with a note encouraging the reader to write his or her own final chapter. This would enable each reader to apply the message of the book to his or her own life and situation. The point she was making was that people must answer for themselves the question, *What do I do with all this?* The purpose of this particular book is certainly not to provide the ultimate answers to the total Christian life. Rather, it is to establish a foundation of hope upon which a durable building can be erected.

What I have been attempting could be described as a *spirituality of hope*. For the nature of the hope we have been exploring is not just an intellectual concept to be grasped (though it must of necessity be that); rather, it is a fundamental truth, a way of seeing and being, which actually grasps us. When we feel that we have grasped hope, we discover that it is we who have been grasped by hope. And this experience is one which motivates, drives, equips, comforts and encourages us. One example from the Bible might help us understand this.

By reputation (or legend), Mary Magdalene was a woman who lived on the seamier side of life. Some think she was a prostitute; and there is some indirect evidence to support this allegation. That she was streetwise and looked down upon by male religious society is probably true. All women were looked down upon by male religious society of that time. However, Mary discovered Jesus to be different from other men: he did not abuse her or take advantage of her, but allowed her not to be imprisoned by her past and her reputation. He gave her the freedom to love and be loved without the threat of being taken for granted or humiliated. Jesus knew what she was like and loved her, responding to her in a way which many (Christian) men would find impossible.

We can only imagine the devastation Mary felt when she stood at the foot of the cross and watched this man die a cruel death. He had given her hope and dignity, he had made the future seem bright and something to look forward to. He had restored to her her sense of self-respect and self-worth. He had shown her what God is like and what sacrificial, selfless love is all about. And now he was dying, and it all seemed too tragic to take in. How could this be happening to this man of all men? Why him? At the foot of that cross, Mary's sense of hope and meaning probably dissolved. We can imagine the sense of disillusionment, anguish, fear and hopelessness. What would happen to her now? Had she been cheated after all?

On the Sunday morning, she went with several other women to the tomb to anoint the body of Jesus. When they got there, the tomb was empty. The figure they saw there, described as an angel, told them not to be afraid. (This seems an odd thing for an angel to say to distraught women who have just had the most unwelcome and confusing shock of their lives.) According to John's Gospel, the resurrected Jesus appears first to Mary Magdalene.

It is significant that, when the male disciples deserted Jesus at his trial, it was the women who did not. All the Gospel writers note the fact that it was the women who watched Jesus die. It was the women who visited the tomb on the Sunday morning. It was the women to whom the resurrected Jesus first appeared. It was the women who ran and told the men about the empty tomb. And it was the men who at first did not believe them.

Mary Magdalene had been through the hell of seeing Jesus crucified and buried. She, of all possible people, was the one who first witnessed the resurrected Jesus. Her hope was restored. Amid the shock and confusion, she experienced the sheer joy of knowing that Jesus had offered a hope for a life that could not be suppressed even by death itself. It had grasped the very fabric of her being, and it would not let her go.

John Bell has captured the emotion of this in a beautiful song called 'Lord of the Morning'.[8] The song begins with Mary Magdalene expressing the dereliction she feels as she approaches the tomb of Jesus on that Sunday morning:

1. I tread on the grass where the dew lies deep
    While the air is clear and the world's asleep;
    I tramp on the verge of a dream that's gone –
    How I miss the Lord of the Morning!
        Morning!
        How can daylight dawn
        Now I miss the Lord of the Morning?

2. I trod through the streets on the resting day,
    Not a soul in sight, not a child at play;
    I tramped on the ash of a fire once bright –
    How I miss the Lord of the Morning!
        Morning!
        Let it still be night,
        For I miss the Lord of the Morning!

3. I trod all the way from the town to the hill
    And I found my way, but I lost my will;
    I tramped up the stairs to a room turned strange –
    How I miss the Lord of the Morning!
        Morning!
        Nothing can derange
        How I miss the Lord of the Morning!

4. I trod out the hours on a wine-stained floor
    Till the darkness warned of the day in store;
    I tramped to a garden, engulfed in dread –
    How I miss the Lord of the Morning!
        Morning!
        Life and love are dead
        And I miss the Lord of the Morning.

In the final verse of the song Jesus responds:

5. I tread on the grass where the dew lies deep
    While the air is clear and the world's asleep;
    I tramp on the verge of an endless dawn –
    For I am the Lord of the Morning,
        Morning!
        Darkness now has gone
        And I am the Lord of the Morning!

HOPING AND PRAYING

This experience of an encounter with the risen Christ is one which prompts us to a deeper longing for his life. Our hunger for him grows as we feed on him, whilst simultaneously being satisfied by him. For to meet with Jesus is to be confronted by hope. To embrace him is to see real life, past, present and future, as being somehow redeemed by him. The still-wounded hands of his resurrection body speak into our pain and suffering. His concern that the disciples should eat a proper breakfast speaks into our daily routine and basic needs.[9]

Having been grasped by hope, we must explore the reality of that hope. And if that hope is found in Jesus, this must mean that we explore him. Our relationship with him and experience of him must deepen and grow as we learn to love him and be loved by him. We will enjoy the freedom of being honest and open with the Jesus who knows us. And, in our times of abandonment, we will be able to trust in the presence of the Jesus who, on his own cross, felt abandoned by God.

The experiences we have been describing throughout this book of repentance, forgiveness and commitment to following Jesus take place in the context of prayer. For it is in prayer that we recognise our nakedness before God and his extravagant love for us. It is in prayer that we perceive the holiness and presence of God. Yet prayer can be the most difficult exercise on earth. It is impossible to pray and at the same time to escape the demands of the one to whom we pray. To enter God's presence in prayer is inevitably to become aware of the need for repentance and change.

The sort of prayer that is all talk and full of words can easily avoid this crisis because it gives no space for God to whisper his truth into the silence of listening minds. If we wish to encounter God in prayer – and there can be no other reason for praying – we have no alternative but to make time and create space from busy lives in order to be silent.

Richard Foster has written:

> To pray is to change. Prayer is the central avenue God uses to transform us. If we are unwilling to change, we will abandon prayer as a noticeable characteristic of our lives. The closer we come to the heartbeat of God the more we see our need and the more we desire to be conformed to Christ.[10]

Once again, the starting point of prayer is the acknowledgement of weakness and need. We have to learn to pray, and we have to practise listening to God. If Richard Foster's understanding of what happens to someone who prays is true, then the learning of it will take more than a lifetime.

> In prayer, real prayer, we begin to think God's thoughts after Him: to desire the things He desires, to love the things

He loves. Progressively we are taught to see things from his point of view.[11]

As a pastor, I have discovered that it is impossible to teach people to pray if they already think they have mastered the art. The evidence is usually to the contrary. I am very pleased for those who find prayer easy and always exciting; but my own experience is of both joy *and* frustration, of ease *and* perseverance. I not only enjoy the loving embrace of the Father, but I also encounter the inescapable call to repentance and change. This is not always comfortable or convenient. But the Bible shows me that I am not alone.

There has to be in every praying Christian a fundamental humility, the knowledge that we have only just begun and that the best is still to come. David Watson wrote of those who respond to God's invitation to hope and to pray in the light of that hope: 'When it comes to prayer there are no experts. We are all children learning from our heavenly Father.'[12]

The implications of this for our individual lives and our corporate life as the Church are far-reaching. To be grasped by hope means living integrated lives with God at the centre. No longer can we split our lives and thinking up into convenient compartments. For, when Jesus is Lord, he will pervade the whole of life and make us very uncomfortable with our weak efforts to avoid him. But to be hopeful is to live a new life of integrity. It is to walk hand in hand with the God of history who alone knows the future. It is to be overwhelmed by the gift of forgiveness and new life, though we deserve neither. To hope is to live for Christ and in Christ. It is also to die for and in Christ.

> 'In the beginning
> You made me;
> Not that you needed to,
> Not that I asked you to,

And you called me to you.
And being me, I said
    "Tomorrow, Lord, tomorrow I will come".
So you gave me a tomorrow,
which is today ...'[13]

NOTES

Chapter 2: Whatever Happened to Hope?

1. Lesslie Newbigin, *The Other Side of 1984* (Geneva: WCC, 1983), p. 1.
2. Obviously the Enlightenment was not the only culprit. Roots are to be found from the Renaissance on. But the Enlightenment was a powerful catalyst in engendering a very significant and comprehensive shift in worldviews.
3. The consequential privatisation of religious faith is possibly the most damaging legacy of Enlightenment thinking. Yet Evangelicalism, often accused of being too individualistic in emphasis, was born of a marriage between serious biblical faith and socioeconomic and political commitment.
4. This is discussed in a paper by Colin A. Russell, 'The Conflict Metaphor and its Social Origins', *Science and Christian Belief,* vol. 1, no. 1 (1989).
5. Many believe the nuclear threat to have disappeared along with Communism in Eastern Europe. This shows the naivety and short-sightedness of untempered optimism.
6. Luke 9:24.
7. Stephen Travis, *I Believe in the Second Coming of Jesus* (London: Hodder, 1982), p. 17. Incidentally, this is an excellent book on the theme of hope.
8. Jacques Ellul, *The Meaning of the City* (Eerdmans, 1970).
9. This idea is taken up again in Chapter 7, 'Hope in the Desert'.

Chapter 3: A History of Hope

1. T. S. Eliot, *Four Quartets, Burnt Norton, I.*

2. Pannenberg does seem to run into logical difficulty here, however. He seems to be identifying God with history. But if God and history are the same thing, what happens to God when history reaches its conclusion – as Pannenberg insists it must?

3. Wolfhart Pannenberg, *Revelation as History* (Sheed & Ward, 1969).

4. See Chapter 6 for expansion of this theme.

5. 1 Corinthians 15:12–19.

6. Jesus used picture language, taught in stories and parables, and stimulated the imagination of his hearers.

7. Genesis 1:27.

8. Genesis 2:15.

9. Helmut Thielicke, *Man in God's World* (London: James Clarke, 1967), p. 85.

10. Colossians 1:20.

11. See Chapter 8: 'Hope in the Face of Death'.

12. Exodus 2 and 3.

13. Exodus 7–15.

14. Exodus 19:24.

15. The first five books of the Old Testament.

16. Jeremiah 7:1–11.

17. Douglas Adams, *The Hitchhiker's Guide to the Galaxy* (London: Pan, 1979).

18. *Freedom is Coming,* Songs of Protest and Praise from South Africa (Utryck, Sweden).

19. Ibid.

20. Isaiah 52:13, 53:1–2.

21. Jeremiah 31:3–14.

22. See John 14.

23. Philippians 1:29–30.

24. Jeremiah was so excited about being a prophet that he often lamented the very fact he had ever been born!

Chapter 4: Hope in the Real World

1. *Enemy of Apathy, Wild Goose Songs* vol. 2 (The Iona Community, Scotland), p. 90.

2. John 1:1–18.

3. Philippians 2:6–8.
4. See, for example, the poems of Wilfred Owen or Siegfried Sassoon.
5. John 7:37.
6. Sir Robert (now Lord) Armstrong, during the Peter Wright *Spycatcher* trial in Australia in 1987.
7. John 8:32–6.
8. Matthew 23:25–8. One charge never brought against Jesus was that he minced his words. He certainly spoke un-ambiguously to those who needed to hear some straight talking.
9. Matthew 5–7.
10. Romans 5:6–8.
11. John 6:35.
12. Mark 8:34–7.
13. Matthew 10:37–9.

Chapter 5: The Roots of Hope

1. Luke 4:14–30.
2. Isaiah 61:1–2 quoted in Luke 4:18–19.
3. Steve Turner, *Hungry for Heaven* (Kingsway/Virgin, 1988).
4. *Strait* (Spring 1990), p. 21.
5. Quoted in David Prior, *Jesus and Power* (London: Hodder, 1987).
6. Micah 6:8. See also Jesus' indictment of religious leaders in Matthew 23:23–4!
7. See James Jones, *Falling into Grace* (London: Daybreak DLT, 1990). This is an excellent and helpful little book on the nature of God's grace.
8. The hymn begins: 'And can it be that I should gain ...'.
9. Ephesians 2:8.
10. Ephesians 2:89.
11. Mark 10:21.

Chapter 6: The Kingdom of Hope

1. Matthew 4:17; Mark 1:15.

2. Jim Wallis, *Agenda for Biblical People* (London: Triangle, 1986), p. 15.
3. Luke 1:50–3.
4. Matthew 5:3–10.
5. Philippians 2:9–11.
6. For example, Matthew 12:28. See also the parables in Matthew 13.
7. For example, Matthew 4:17.
8. For example, Luke 17:20–1.
9. For example, Matthew 25:34.
10. John 14:15–27.
11. Matthew 5–7.
12. Ephesians 2:14–18.
13. James 2:14–24.
14. John 13:1–17, 15:9–17.
15. See Jim Wallis' experience in Jim Wallis, *The New Radical* (Lion). See also *The Call to Conversion* (Lion, 1981).
16. All these are to be found in Matthew 13:31–50.
17. Matthew 20:1–16.
18. See Samson and David, for example.
19. Luke 12:9.
20. Cf. Peter's experiences in Acts 10 and 11; Galatians 2:11–21.
21. 'Take this Moment', *Love from Below, Wild Goose Songs* vol. 3 (The Iona Community, Glasgow), p. 86.

Chapter 7: Hope in the Desert

1. Francis Schaeffer, *The God Who is There* (Hodder, 1968).
2. The whole story is recounted in the book of Exodus.
3. Kosuke Koyama, *Three Mile an Hour God* (SCM, 1979), p. 3.
4. Ibid., p. 4.
5. Matthew 3:13–4:11.
6. Hebrews 4:15. See also Hebrews 2:14–18.
7. This episode perhaps ought not to be called *the temptation* of Jesus, as if it were the only such time he faced it. His experience in Gethsemane was fairly grim.
8. Psalm 42.

Chapter 8: Hope in the Face of Death

1. Of course, each person's actual death can only be experienced by the one who dies. But the event of the death is shared by, and affects, many people in different ways.
2. Philippe Ariès, *Western Attitudes Toward Death* (Baltimore: John Hopkins University Press, 1974).
3. Ibid., p. 85.
4. L. N. Tolstoy, *The Death of Ivan Ilyich* (Penguin, 1960).
5. Ariès, op. cit., pp. 88f.
6. Quoted in Travis, op. cit., p. 163.
7. Ariès, op. cit., p. 94.
8. I do not wish to trivialise the ethical problem here. But I do want to say that it is an ethical problem. Cold statistics do suggest something about our priorities and values.
9. Geoffrey Gorer, *Death, Grief and Mourning in Contemporary Britain* (London: Cresset Press, 1965).
10. Genesis 2:7.
11. See, for example, Psalm 139.
12. There are many books available which deal with the evidence for the resurrection. One of the best is still Frank Morrison, *Who Moved the Stone?* (London: Faber, 1958). Also see Colin Chapman, *The Case for Christianity* (Tring: Lion, 1981) and N. T. Wright, *The Resurrection of the Son of God* (London: SPCK, 2003).
13. John 11:25–6.
14. Philippians 1:21.
15. John 11:1–44.
16. Helmut Thielicke, *Christ and the Meaning of Life* (London: James Clarke, 1965), p. 18.
17. See Daniel 3:16–18 for the attitude of Shadrach, Meshach and Abednego.
18. William Barclay, *A New Testament Wordbook* (London: SCM, 1955), p. 120.
19. Quoted in Travis, op. cit., p. 218.
20. Mary Bosanquet, *The Life and Death of Dietrich Bonhoeffer* (Hodder, 1968), p. 277.
21. John de Gruchy, *Cry Justice: Prayers, meditations and readings from South Africa* (Collins, 1986), p. 80.

22. The New Testament letters contain moving accounts of dreadful suffering. For example, see Paul's account in 2 Corinthians 10–13.
23. Romans 8:31–9.

Chapter 9: Hoping and Praying

1. Hubert G. Locke (ed.), *Exile in the Fatherland*, Martin Niemöller's Letters from Moabit Prison (Grand Rapids: Eerdmans, 1986).
2. See Isaiah 64:8.
3. See Bonhoeffer's uncompromising study of grace and discipleship in Dietrich Bonhoeffer, *The Cost of Discipleship* (London: SCM, 1980).
4. For example, Psalms 73, 74.
5. For example, Psalm 43.
6. 1 Samuel 16:7.
7. For an excellent account of the nature of grace and forgiveness, see James Jones, *Falling into Grace* (London: DLT, 1990).
8. *Enemy of Apathy, Wild Goose Songs* vol. 2 (The Iona Community, Scotland), p. 62.
9. John 21:1–14.
10. Richard Foster, *Celebration of Discipline* (London: Hodder, 1983), p. 30.
11. Ibid.
12. David Watson, *Discipleship* (London: Hodder, 1981), p. 121. The section on prayer in this book is simple, practical and very helpful.
13. From a litany 'Morning Comes', *The Iona Community Worship Book* (Wild Goose Publications, 1988), p. 77.